The Sounds of the Sixties and the Church

To Mark

best wishes

Stephen Wright

by

Stephen Wright

**Grosvenor House
Publishing Limited**

This book is published by
Grosvenor House Publishing Ltd
28-30 High Street, Guildford, Surrey, GU1 3HY.
www.grosvenorhousepublishing.co.uk

A CIP record for this book
is available from the British Library

ISBN 978-1-906645-27-4

To
Helen Margaret Wright
(1962-2004)

Contents

Acknowledgements

This work was written and researched following the death of my wife in 2004. It is, therefore, something amounting to a minor miracle that it ever saw the light of day at all. That it has appeared is due to a large number of people who I am only too happy to acknowledge here. The Methodist Church, largely through the auspices of the Reverend Tom Stuckey, allowed me time to study, and, eventually to present this work to Surrey University for the award of MPhil. I was privileged to encounter an array of Christian musicians who were remarkably willing to answer my questions, most notably Tim Anderson, Peter Banks, Chris Bowater, Eddie Boyes, Neil Burnham, Charles Cleall, Tony Goodman, Garth Hewitt, Roger Hurrell, Ishmael, Judy MacKenzie Dunn, Derrick Phillips and Peter D. Smith. To these should be added Ed Nadorozny and Ken Scott, non-musicians, their passion for early electric Christian music is unrivalled, their willingness to help me in my quest humbling. I was also extremely fortunate to have Tina Beattie and Philip Richter as my MPhil supervisors, their ideas, patience and encouragement is fundamental to all that follows, though not it should be added, any short comings in my argument. Alongside these clergy, musicians, scholars and journalists, thanks must go to many Christian friends whose encouragement was invaluable during the preparation of this work. Some like Wendy Lucas, Fran Logan and Fleur Chambers became extended members of the Wright family. Finally, deep gratitude must go to my parents for their love and support, and last but not least, to my two boys, Gregory and Michael, whose zest for life kept me going in difficult times.

Preface

My personal recollection of 1960s music is rather vague. This is not I hasten to add because I was 'high' on drugs and alcohol at the time, (the almost routine comical jibe that is given for being there but not remembering). Rather, in the rock 'n' roll parlance of the 1970s rock band Mott the Hoople, I was 'Born too late '58'. My teenage years were the 1970s and I was an enthusiastic consumer of the youth music of that era. I preferred the more 'serious' sounds of Roxy Music, Barclay James Harvest, Focus, Alice Cooper, Yes and the Eagles to the pop songs of the charts. Although some of my favourite groups sold a lot of singles I was mainly interested in albums. When I became a Christian in my middle teens it never occurred to me that I should give up my love of contemporary music. Indeed, one of my memories of 1960s church life was of a beat band, who on a few occasions, came to our village chapel and performed with their electric guitars. It wasn't long before I followed in their footsteps and helped create a band which was determined to present the message of Jesus in a way that young people could understand. It was an exciting period; the contemporary Christian music scene was making great advances, along with secular artists, I now found room for overtly Christian sounds, including the likes of Larry Norman and Randy Stonehill from America and British talent such as The Mighty Flyers, Bryn Haworth, Garth Hewitt and After the Fire. As a young adult my entire social life revolved around the band of which I was member and journeying to watch other Christian performers.

Having an experience of faith and youth music which was grounded in the 1970s, the process by which I came to write about Christians and the youth music of the 1960s is long and complex. A key point came when I observed that a number of social historians appeared to suggest that the traditional churches were universally damning of 1960s youth music. If this were true I could not understand how the Christian music scene of which I was a part in the 1970s could ever have developed. Contemporary Christian youth music did not just appear *ex nihilo*, ready formed; it grew and evolved out of the 1960s. Many of the Christian artists I admired were inspired by the pop and rock of that period. The same was true of the band in which I played and we also performed Christian material which was first published in the 1960s. I knew from personal experience that there were those in the 1970s who thought that Christianity and secular youth music ought not to mix. It seemed inevitable that the same was true a decade earlier. But if the rejection of new musical trends during the 1960s was as severe and as universal as certain critics had suggested, then it was difficult to account for my teenage experience in which contemporary music played such a large part. This work will suggest that these impressions were not unfounded and that the 1960s church was far from being entirely negative in its response to youth music.

As I will show, some Christians undoubtedly regarded modern youth sounds as 'the devil's music', but others were prepared to reject such descriptions and rejoined with the phrase 'Why should the devil have all the good music?' The origin of these words is uncertain (they have been attributed to Luther, Calvin, John and Charles Wesley and William Booth) but they were used to indicate that the church should be prepared to use secular music in its worship and mission (Westermeyer, 1998:288). Indeed, in its readiness to appropriate new music parts of the church shared something of that creative, adventurous spirit, so characteristic of the 1960s. What is beyond doubt is that this pioneering use of pop, folk and rock has seldom been acknowledged or given much credence within the British churches. In particular, the contribution of British

Christian pop and rock artists has either been derided as second rate or forgotten about entirely in favour of Christian artists from America. In the early years of a new millennium, it is high time that the pioneering work of Christian artists of the 1960s is properly acknowledged. I hope this volume goes some way towards making that possible.

Introduction

This study will show that there was a variety of Christian reactions to 1960s youth music and whether it was suitable for use within the church. The main argument will suggest, against certain social historians, that there was a willingness on the part of many church people to be creatively engaged with the new youth sounds. In a more general way it will also attempt to show who was involved in this interface between church and culture. It will suggest that this was not the total preserve of modern minded church leaders desperate to be 'with it', but involved the talents and skills of both lay and ordained.

Social Historians, Church and Youth Music

The number of studies which look at the issue of ecclesiastical responses to 1960s youth music is not large. References are often assimilated within larger studies which focus on the entire phenomenon of opposition to pop and rock music. Three typical examples which will feature in the following are *Anti-rock* by Linda Martin and Kerry Segrave, *Banned!* by Martin Cloonan and *Shock waves: The authoritative response to popular music* by John Street. Other references can be found in social histories of youth culture such as John Davis' *Youth and the Condition of Britain* and more general historical accounts of the period. But the most detailed discussions are to be found within the general treatments of opposition to youth music. This in itself presents a difficulty for anyone wanting a realistic impression of Christian attitudes because the focus of these studies majors on negative opinions. This is especially the case with

Martin and Segrave and Cloonan. It was not part of their brief to draw attention to the acceptance and embrace of pop and rock. There were qualifications that these authors provided, for example Martin and Segrave admit that much of the opposition to youth music came from Christian fundamentalists, in other words from one extreme part of the Christian constituency (Segrave, Martin, 1993:181ff). Cloonan reflects a similar perspective, after discussing the 1960s he writes: 'By 1967 the battle lines between pop and *sections* of organised religion had been drawn' (Cloonan, 1996: 237, my italics). Again, having noted some Christian criticism of youth music in the 1970s, he admits that these were 'isolated outbursts' and that only 'some' clerics thought rock music should be approached with caution (Cloonan, 1996:238). Such qualifying statements, however, were not a prominent feature of these studies. There is little hint of Christian acceptance, let alone engagement and appropriation. The overriding impression is of a reactionary, critical church unwilling to affirm musical innovations.

The picture of a church largely critical of youth music is not without problems. If the preoccupation with oppositional viewpoints is a weakness there are at least two other methodological weaknesses. The first concerns the limited range of examples or sources on which it is based. Scholars provide remarkably few examples of the church in Great Britain opposing the new music of the 1960s. John Street, who investigates the furore surrounding the award of the MBE to the Beatles, has nothing to say on the matter (Street, 1992: 302-324). Martin and Segrave refer to the trenchant criticisms of the musician Charles Cleall (Martin and Segrave, 1993:177-178). Despite making reference to John Lennon's comment that the Beatles were more popular than Jesus, Cloonan provides no evidence of concern by Christians in the United Kingdom. He is however able to cite earlier opposition to the Beatles and also refers to two other minor controversies, but in only one of these is it clear that there was any church comment (Cloonan, 1996:237). Yet, as was shown earlier, he can still imagine the church embroiled in a

2

battle with pop and rock. The limited amount of data which support such a conclusion, suggests that more is at work here than careful analysis. So, how is it possible that scholars have been able to draw such grand conclusions from such small amounts of evidence?

One possible explanation of historians' perceptions is that earlier Christian criticism of youth music in the 1950s came to be seen as the template of all church attitudes, enabling them to prescribe what church reactions might be. The advent of rock 'n' roll certainly did worry some Christians and the evidence for this would appear to be more extensive and thorough going than that of the 1960s. But even here, the citations that scholars provide can hardly be described as large. In fact, one of the few positive church stories comes from this period. John Davis reports a moderate clerical view in the wake of the furore surrounding the emergence of rock 'n' roll (Davis, 1990:163). More illustrative of the relative shortage of critical material is the fact that scholars recycle oppositional comments. For example, a Pentecostal pastor from Nottingham who is said to have connected rock 'n' roll with the devil, lawlessness and immorality appears in Cloonan, Davis, Martin and Segrave and Street (Cloonan, 1996:236, Davis, 1990:163, Martin and Seagrave, 1993:49, Street, 1992:305). A letter of the Bishop of Woolwich in which he suggested that rhythm might have 'a maddening effect' on young people and reduce their self control is likewise reported in all but Street (Cloonan, 1996:235-236, Davis, 1990:163-164, Martin and Seagrove, 1993:35). Two other British examples that are offered by Martin and Seagrave, the views of a Reverend J. H. Chamberlain of Smethwick and Dr Donald Soper, are also reproduced by Cloonan and the latter has nothing original to report. Street alone records that the Moral Welfare Council of the Church of England was 'concerned' about the 'damage' rock 'n' roll songs might do (Street, 1992:305). Although ultimately limited in number, these stories and comments may have been understood to be determinative of church reactions, with the consequence that little elaboration of the theme was felt necessary a few years later.

A further explanation of the perception that Christians were opposed to the new musical developments of the 1960s, despite lack of extensive evidence, may have something to do with scholars' own perceptions of the suitability of such music for Christian use. For example, in an earlier work John Street developed the theme that for music to 'work', a kind of harmony was needed between the character of the message and the nature of the music. One of the examples he gives of this is the incongruence of rock music and religion. He suggested that there is little 'common ground' between the world of faith and the world of rock.

> Rock's focus is on the individual, its sexual imagery is concerned with male conquest and adolescent angst, and its obsession is the moment and immediate gratification. Religion offers sacrifice and redemption (deferred gratification), and regards sex with suspicion. The integration of Protestantism into popular music requires more than the addition of suitably reverential lyrics because the whole character of the music seems to work against the ways of worship. Or to put it the other way around, rock only allows for certain kinds of ideas and attitudes.
>
> (Street, 1986:71-72)

Interestingly, this has similarities with the Christian critics of the 1960s who argued that youth music was inappropriate for church use because of its immoral associations. In this case, Street's argument is weakened by the narrow way in which he defined the parameters of rock and religion. Indeed, his own analysis revealed that rock and pop had wider horizons than the above quotation suggests. He discusses the yearning for something more, what others have called 'the urge for the transcendence', (Frisckics-Warren, 2005), concerns about injustice and the way the world is for example (Street, 1986:193ff). His summary of religion in the quotation above is equally truncated and also appears to be questioned by his own work. In his discussion of gospel music for example, he acknowledges that religion is concerned with 'celebration' and 'ecstasy'. In other words, it is not just about sacrifice and a deferred redemption. Whatever one might make of Street's analysis, the key point for my argument is that he is not sympathetic to the idea that Christians can fuse faith and youth music in a fruitful way. It is possible that this kind of predisposition has affected his understanding of the relationship between Christianity and modern music, yielding a bias towards critical Christian comments rather than positive ones, and perhaps making it easier to assume that the negative opinions of the 1950s represented the default position of the traditional churches.

Whether in respect to the 1950s or the 1960s youth music, the image of the church as essentially antagonistic is based on a relatively small number of (usually extreme) statements. The second methodological problem is related to this in that it appears that the picture of an unsympathetic church was generated from largely secular sources. This is especially noticeable in the treatments of 1950s youth music where the majority of cited comments are derived from the *Melody Maker* or *The Times*. Although the small amount of 1960s material is a little more diverse, secular sources still predominate. For example, the most comprehensive treatment of the British music scene is by Cloonan who quotes from a journal article by Street and his two minor controversy stories mentioned above are both sourced from the *Melody Maker*. The reliance on secular sources may well indicate why scholars are able to offer only a small number of examples of church attitudes. Quite clearly, *The Melody Maker,* for example, was not a magazine which was devoted to the musical tastes of religious people. Christian opinions on youth music cannot have appeared very regularly. The dependence on secular sources might also suggest why scholars tend to report only critical voices. By the criteria of newsworthiness, controversial statements by a clergy person rated much more highly than any hypothetical Christian appropriation of youth music. Consequently, it is the negative comments that dominate the headlines and eventually influence scholarly studies. The infrequency of comments and the reproduction of negative material inevitably raise serious questions about the usefulness of secular sources in this matter. Beyond the fairly elementary fact that certain church people were opposed to pop and rock, it has yielded little. It would certainly be most unwise to imply some kind of general church hostility towards pop and rock on this basis. Yet this is exactly what has been done.

Different but Similar

One author who stands apart from those mentioned above is Dominic Sandbrook. In the second of his two volume account of the 1960s, his presentation of the church and of clergy contrasts sharply with those of Cloonan, Martin and Segrave and Street. He develops the theme of a church leadership determined to appear modern, relevant and trendy (Sandbrook, 2006:433ff). The main application of this is the controversy surrounding Dr John Robinson, the Bishop of Woolwich. Sandbrook explains how the Bishop's famous book *Honest to God* challenged Christians to rethink their image of God and their morality. Either side of this discourse the theme of 'vicars striving desperately to appear culturally relevant' is progressed with reference to music (Sandbrook, 2006:433). The Bishop of Coventry is quoted as looking forward to 'experiments' in 'new-look worship' (Sandbrook, 2006:433). Sandbrook also recounts a televised broadcast in which the Archbishop of York, Donald Coggan, was interviewed by the singer Adam Faith. The Archbishop maintained that he was 'all for' rewriting classic hymns so that the young could understand them (Sandbrook, 2006:433). Later, the author notes that it was during the 1960s that 'churchmen began wielding guitars, introducing handclapping into the Anglican rite and generally conducting themselves like frustrated pop stars' (Sandbrook, 2006:439). Such language reflects the fact that Sandbrook is not particularly comfortable with such developments. Indeed, he argues that they were partly responsible for the decline of church attendance during this period (Sandbrook, 2006:439). He draws attention to the common stereotype of the 'trendy vicar' and how attempts at modernisation were commonly ridiculed, not least because they were 'laughably inept' (Sandbrook, 2006:433, 439).

Sandbrook's account highlights once again how personal prejudice and predisposition can affect judgements. His dislike of vicars 'wielding guitars' is scarcely concealed and his readiness to associate this with church decline is as questionable, and certainly as unprovable, as Street's objection to the fusion of faith and rock on the grounds that they shared no common ground. At the same time, Sandbrook's presentation provides a much needed correction to those historians who have concluded that the church offered only critical assessments of youth music. The themes of church engagement and appropriation hinted at in Sandbrook's brief treatment will be more fully explored in this study. Indeed, it is the limited nature of Sandbrook's piece which makes it most vulnerable to criticism.

Perhaps the most obvious limitation of Sandbrook's piece is that there is no reference to dissenting voices. In the failure to acknowledge any opposition to the new music and its use by the church, Sandbrook's account can be accused of being as one sided as those by scholars mentioned above. His brief treatment can also be accused of causing confusion. By presenting musical innovation as part of a wider modernising movement, including the work of those like Bishop Robinson, he creates the impression that the same Christians were involved in the reshaping of both theology and music. The prefacing of his comment about churchmen wielding guitars with the word 'liberal' would seem to reinforce this idea. It is possible of course, that Sandbrook is using the word 'liberal' in a general sense, as someone not bound by tradition and open to new ideas, in which case a wide category of musical innovators is in mind. But the word 'liberal' might also be understood to refer specifically to free thinking theologians. Lack of detail makes the precise meaning unclear, but if he is suggesting that the theological liberals were at the forefront of an engagement with youth culture he is in error. It was evangelicals who most engaged with youth music. Another major weakness is the focus on clergy. Sandbrook gives the impression that it was they who were mainly responsible for moving the church in a modern musical direction. As leaders of Christian communities they were obviously influential but the story of the churches' engagement with youth music is, as I shall show, not just a story of the 'trendy vicar' behaving like a 'frustrated pop star'. It was commonly a 'grass roots' movement involving Christian young people who desired to communicate faith in a way that was relevant for their generation. Sandbrook's failure to appreciate this can be explained, once again, by a reliance on secular sources. Newspapers like the *Observer* or the *Guardian* and, indeed, BBC television, all of which are cited by Sandbrook, were understandably interested in what churchmen said and did; they were inevitably less interested in the activities of the average churchgoer or indeed of Christian young people. The place of clergy was lionised and their views given priority. For historians who are over reliant on such sources there is a consequent risk of reflecting this clerical primacy as if they represented the entire church. In suggesting that church leaders were mainly responsible for the development of new trends in music and faith in the 1960s it seems that Sandbrook may be guilty of this.

The purpose of my study is to provide a more nuanced and comprehensive analysis of Christian responses to youth music in the 1960s. In undertaking this research, I draw upon existing studies but engage with a range of additional primary sources in order to challenge some of the conclusions of Sandbrook, Martin and Segrave, Cloonan and Street.

Methodology

To ensure that the project did not become unwieldy, the focus falls upon the traditional Protestant churches in the United

Kingdom. It is their response to youth music that is examined and not for example, those of the Pentecostal churches or the Roman Catholic community. Dramatic changes were taking place within this latter constituency during the 1960s, but the impact of Vatican II and wider cultural changes upon its music will not be explored here.

The study extends beyond the strict confines of the seventh decade of the twentieth century. This is not because of any theoretical view about when the 1960s truly began and ended as seen in certain historical studies concerned with periodisation, such as those by Marwick and Sandbrook. It is simply to recognise that it is impossible to appreciate the youth music of the 1960s without placing it in its social and musical context. At the same time any assessment of the impact of 1960s youth music on churchgoers inevitably extends beyond that decade. Such has been the influence of the Beatles, Bob Dylan and Jimi Hendrix for example, that a very much larger work could have been written extending right up to present times. This study has a more limited sphere of interest. Its main focus centres on how Christians engaged with 1960s styles during that decade and the 1970s. The final chapter, which concerns the decline of Christian engagement with contemporary styles, covers the period from the 1970s to the end of the millennium.

The research is grounded, unlike the work of the scholars above, in an examination of primary church sources. These include personal interviews, song books, vinyl records, information available on web sites and books. At the heart of this work has been an examination of certain Christian newspapers over the period. Four of these were chosen to evaluate a cross section of Christian opinion. The best known are probably the *Church Times* and the *Methodist Recorder*. These represent the middle ground and establishment and nonconformist views respectively. From the conservative wing of the church the *Christian Herald* was chosen. Strongly protestant and royalist, it regularly featured a column by the evangelist Billy Graham. At the other end of the theological spectrum was *New Christ-*

ian. This began publication in October 1965 and only just survived the birth of the next decade before it ceased publication. Its significance lies in that it represented the kind of progressive, radical opinion synonymous with Dr Robinson. Indeed, he was a regular contributor (Beeson, *New Christian*, 07 October 1965:21). The results of this analysis are concentrated in the chapter 'The Discontents', but material is also to be found elsewhere, most notably in the chapters on pop and on folk music. It should be noted that when reference is made to 'the Christian press' it is these four magazines that are meant.

In this chapter I have already made reference to 'pop', 'rock', 'contemporary music', 'new music' and 'youth music'. Any work of this kind inevitably has to struggle with what is meant by these terms. Indeed, any reader has a right to know what kind of music I am discussing when I consider church reactions to it. I should make it clear then, that the subject of this study is that which is probably best described as youth music. As the following chapter will indicate the birth of rock 'n' roll gave rise to a sense that certain types of music were closely associated with teenagers and young people. This trend continued in the 1960s, but it does not mean that older adults were excluded entirely from this spectacle. The Beatles for example, appealed to a wide range of people, including older church people. An elderly correspondent of the *Methodist Recorder* admitted to her love of classical music but also confessed: 'I love beat and pop music too' (Lumley, *Methodist Recorder*, 30 April 1964:14). Nevertheless, music which was performed by young people and mainly consumed by young people inevitably was perceived to be intimately associated with young people. Identifying the subject of my study in this way does not immediately resolve all matters of definition however.

One of the most important issues of classification concerns two key words which are used to describe the sounds of youth music, namely 'pop' and 'rock'. There are those who do not distinguish between the two and use either word to describe the entire youth music phenomenon (Shuker, 1994:6ff). In many ways this is understandable. In recent decades, the fusion of different musical genres has produced a bewildering diversity which makes definition difficult. Even in the 1960s, in a simpler musical age, attempting to define what constituted 'pop' and 'rock' is far from easy. The work of the later Beatles illustrates the problem. Richard Buskin for example, categorised their classic 1967 album, *Sgt. Pepper's Lonely Heart Club Band* as rock, while Iain Chambers, though acknowledging its pushing of conventions, described it as pop (Buskin, 2003:80-81, Chambers, 1985:99). Certain examples of 1960s youth music are notoriously difficult to categorise, especially as (reflected in the case of the Beatles) pop sensibilities began to move towards a rock style. It is also complicated by the fact that artists themselves produced songs in a variety of genres. In Christian terms this is illustrated by the duo Malcolm and Alwyn who in only two albums, not only produced fusions of folk with pop and rock, but also stand alone pop and rock songs. Despite the difficulties involved in categorising musical styles and artists, I believe it is still possible to isolate differences. By the end of the 1960s, the distinction between pop and rock was commonly made and this study will affirm that perception (Chambers, 1985:116-117). In the following chapter, which briefly recounts the story of 1960s youth music, attention is drawn to some of rock music's defining characteristics. These are essentially musical and not concerned with any notions of authenticity which have often been claimed by rock performers and their fans for their music. The contrast between the commercial, manufactured nature of pop and the creative artist, sublimely expressing themselves through music, was a central part of the ideology of rock (Frith and Horne, 1987:88ff). Any historical account cannot ignore this aspect because the notion of rock as high art helped shape the music itself. But special claims to authenticity are not endorsed here. Rock music was just as concerned with commercial realities as main stream pop and it is by no means clear that the latter was totally devoid of creativity (Frith, 1983:130ff). In this study then, 'pop' and 'rock' distinctions are attempted on a musical basis rather than on any claims to special musical status.

One final issue that requires explanation is the decision to include folk music within the general category of youth sounds. Unlike some of the electric music of the 1960s, folk music cannot be regarded as a novel departure for western audiences. Indeed, those involved in the post war folk revival made much of its associations with the past. Yet, as will be seen, the emergence of Bob Dylan gave folk music a prominence not seen before and an appreciative youthful audience. Dylan became an iconic figure and shared centre stage with the likes of the Beatles and the Rolling Stones. An emphasis upon the latter's meteoric rise can allow the popularity of folk music and the fusion of folk and rock that followed to be overlooked. But the attention that the music press gave this phenomenon highlights the contribution it made to the youth spectacle of the times. This is conveniently represented in an issue of the *NME Originals* series of magazines which is dedicated to Dylan and the folk rock boom of 1964 to 1974 (*NME Originals*, Vol.2, Issue 5). The magazine consists of interviews and reviews taken from *The New Musical Express*, *Disc Weekly* and *Melody Maker* and illustrates how folk not only occupied interior columns of youth music magazines but also their front pages. There was for example, a great deal of interest in Dylan's character, his connection with the British artist Donovan and his relationship with Joan Baez (*NME Originals*, Vol.2, Issue 5:10-25). It seems entirely appropriate then to consider the traditional churches response to this kind of youth music as well as pop and rock.

An Outline

This exploration of Christian responses to 1960s youth music, begins (as has been previously mentioned), with a brief outline in chapter one of the emergence of youth culture and the development of musical styles. The following three chapters explore how Christians responded in a positive way to the new music. I adopt a chronological approach, focussing on particular styles as they came to prominence in church circles. This can only be a general schema but it does appear that the Beatles' beat style featured strongly in the early to middle part of the 1960s, that folk became popular during the second half of decade and that appropriations of rock appeared towards its end. That this is only a rough approximation is evident, for example, in that Christian folk singers were performing during the period when the popularity of beat was at its height. As a broad outline, however, I believe it does reflect the order in which certain youth music styles became popular within the church. Consequently, chapter two focuses on the pop music of the beat boom. It shows how the arrival of the Beatles impacted upon the worshipping life of churches across the country in the form of so called 'beat services'. I draw attention to the appropriation of beat by evangelicals who pioneered the use of electric youth music as a means of evangelisation. Chapter three recounts the popularity of folk music and considers why it had such widespread acceptance within the church. Chapters four and five look at more controversial styles. The focus of chapter four is the emergence and growth of Christian rock music. I consider the motivational factors which encouraged Christian artists to take their music to secular venues. Chapter five considers the opposition to these developments and notes that criticism was far from universal. Indeed, I argue that by the end of the 1960s the prospects for youth music within the church looked good, chapter six offers possible explanations as to why those prospects were not realised. The brief final chapter, attempts to answer the 'so what?' question. Drawing on my analysis of the 1960s it indicates what I perceive to be the lessons for the contemporary church.

1

Musical Revolution

The emergence of youth music in the 1960s cannot be properly understood without reference to wider social and political developments, or to the musical trends which preceded the decade. These contextual concerns are at the heart of this brief account of the development of 1960s pop, folk and rock. In particular, it highlights the growing importance of youth as a distinct group within society and how fusions of different styles of music became a distinguishing feature of the musical revolution.

Revolution

There can be few words more commonly associated with the 1960s than revolution. What is meant by this frequently used adjective varies considerably. At various points certain groups presented themselves as agents of social and political change, culminating in the student protests of the second half of the decade. Commentators frequently identify culture as the hub of the changes that occurred in the 1960s and focus on factors such as the transformation in 'material conditions, lifestyles, family relationships and personal freedoms' (Marwick, 1998:15). Others point to an underlying transformation of attitude and outlook, a 'Revolution in the head', which usually involved a move away from traditional Christian values (MacDonald, 1994:24ff, Brown, 2001:5ff, 175ff). Whether one imagines the 1960s to be characterized by visions of societal transformation, cultural change, new perspectives on reality, or any combina-

1 5

tion of these, there was also another significant revolution which marked the decade. The decade saw an immense change in popular music. In the early 1950s, popular music was dominated by middle of the road, family entertainment which reflected the world of show business (Frith, 1983:32ff). Iain Chamber's analysis of the two leading music papers of the period, *Melody Maker* and *New Musical Express,* revealed a music scene awash with 'impresarios', 'musical standards' and 'tuneful melodies' (Chambers, 1985:19). This scenario was disturbed by the advent of rock 'n' roll in 1956. By the end of the decade, this rebellious youth music had been toned down to such an extent that in many cases there was little to distinguish it from the well crafted show business songs of earlier times (Frith, 1983:33). But things were about to change. The musical revolution of the 1960s brought an end to musical stability. By the end of the decade, well respected serious music, like jazz, had declined dramatically, traditional music, like folk, had been revitalised and new music, like beat, blues and rock had taken centre stage. The fusion of different musical styles was bewildering. Moreover, the associations of pop music with family entertainment had been severed. There remained a vibrant market for music with a wide ranging appeal; it is often forgotten that the 1960s were boom times for the soundtrack LP. Albums such as *The Sound of Music* and *Mary Poppins* sold in vast quantities (Harker, 1992:241). But pop was now intrinsically linked with youth.

The Emergence of Youth

The years following the Second World War saw the rise of youth as a unique and distinct category, set apart from older generations. This was not an entirely novel departure. As Bill Osgerby's study of *Youth in Britain Since 1945* reveals, the modern notion of youth as a particular stage in human development, which begins with puberty and ends in mature adulthood came to be fixed during the late Victorian and Edwardian eras. During this time there were precursors of later 'youth culture', including a youth driven leisure market and dress style (Osgerby, 1998:18-19). In the first half of the twentieth century, the most familiar image of youth style came from 1920s America and its associations with jazz and style. The 'Roaring Twenties' saw the emergence of radical lifestyles among more affluent young people (Davis, 1990:81). During the same period, a thriving working class youth culture existed in the United Kingdom centred on the commercial dance hall (Davis, 1990:81). Nevertheless, the post war years marked a period when the visibility of youth and its differentiation from other generations were to reach new levels. Osgerby's study offers a number of key factors which helped increase the categorization of youth as a distinct entity. These he identifies as:

(a) Demography: The post war baby boom meant that the numbers of young grew in both absolute numbers and as a percentage of the population.
(b) Institutionalization: The raising of the school age to fifteen in 1944 and increasing educational expansion meant that it was possible to identify youth as a 'discrete generational category'. The expansion of the Youth Service in creating leisure facilities for young people had a similar impact.
(c) National Service: This further lengthened out the period of youth, as conscripts could not join until they were eighteen and led to an unsettled hiatus between leaving school and joining up. Osgerby also suggests that conscription, which ended in 1960, might also have increased a sense of 'generational consciousness' among young men and a sharing of different youth cultures (Osgerby, 1998:18ff).

Important as these factors were in highlighting youth as a distinct category, economic factors were, if anything, even more crucial.

In 1957, the Conservative Prime Minister, Harold Macmillan, uttered his famous remark that the British people had 'never had it so good'. It reflected that in comparison with the austerity of the immediate post-war period, the 1950s saw a significant growth in living standards. With full employment, low taxes and the new easy availability of hire purchase, successive Conservative governments helped create a consumer boom. An increasing number of households began to enjoy ownership of washing machines, vacuum cleaners, televisions, cars and other domestic appliances. The rise in living standards was reflected in the rise of young people with money to spend. Youth benefited from their parent's affluence, but young people of employable age also gained from a growing demand for unskilled and semi-skilled workers. The expansion of production line technologies associated with the manufacture of consumer durables meant that there were immediate rewards for young people who were willing to undertake such work (Frith, 1983:36, Osgerby, 1998:22-24). The first major youth cultural phenomenon of the 1950s, the Teddy boy, broadened out in this context. Originating in the working class districts of south and east London, it spread to other, mainly urban areas, as the decade progressed (Davis, 199:143). The Ted's distinctive dress involved drape jackets, drain pipe trousers, thick crepe soled shoes ('brothel creepers') and sculptured Brylcream hair styles (Chambers, 1985:25-26). This flamboyant sartorial style suggested that youthful consumption, unlike that of their parents, was based on leisure rather than the household. But it is with the more general term of 'teenager', (a word invented in America in the late 1940s or early 1950s and quickly adopted in the United Kingdom), that youth became properly associated with a 'conspicuous, leisure-orientated consumption' (Osgerby, 1998:35, Bradley, 1992:84). The image of affluent teenagers spending money according to their own tastes and interests became a dominant motif of the 1950s and 1960s media. It was a theme which was reflected in three important texts which appeared during 1959-60. Mark Abrams' market survey, *The Teenage Consumer*, Colin MacInnes' novel, *Absolute Beginners* and an Education White Paper on the Youth Service, usually referred to as 'The Albermarle Report', 'trumpeted' the arrival of affluent youth (Marwick, 1998:41-42). More recent analysis has attempted to add greater nuance to the picture of young people that is presented in these works. Usually by acknowledging that there were wide regional variations in the degree to which youth benefited from the consumer boom (Bradley, 1992:85, Osgerby, 1998:25-26). Nevertheless, it remains the case that economic success did impinge on many young lives in a positive way, most notably in creating a period of 'relative prosperity' for working class youth (Osgerby, 1998:26).

Rock 'n' Roll

A notable component of youth consumption was music. According to Abrams' 1959 survey, teenagers spending accounted for forty four per cent of total spending on records (Osgerby, 1998:24). Abrams' rather strange definition of teenager, as those between the ages of fifteen and twenty five and unmarried, inevitably distorted the extent to which genuine teenagers bought records. Nevertheless, it highlighted the importance of the general youth market to the record industry. At the beginning of the 1950s, this market was still to flourish. But it was encouraged by the introduction of the seven inch, 45 r.p.m. single in 1952. It was a medium especially attractive to young people, being cheap, easily transportable and almost indestructible (Shuker, 1994:42-43). In America, the low distribution costs associated with the new 45's, allowed small, independent record labels to compete and have hit records. It was one of these, Sun Records, which introduced the world to Elvis Presley, who along with Bill Haley, Buddy Holly and others, were to provide a distinctive musical sound which youth would make their own.

In Britain, it was Bill Haley and the Comets who first established a 'preliminary definition' and a sense of rock 'n' roll musical style (Bradley, 1992:55). By the time that Presley began to make an impact in the United Kingdom, in the spring of 1956, Haley had already achieved chart success. In many ways, he was a most unlikely youth idol, nearing thirty, balding, portly and chubby faced, he lacked the physical appeal of the conventional musical celebrity. Nevertheless, his music attracted a youthful musical audience which included Teddy boys, who so took to Haley and early rock 'n' roll that they became quintessentially associated with the style (Davis, 1990:164-165). The loud guitar and drum based sound did not appeal to parents, and the sense of musical polarization between the generations was underlined by the film 'Rock Around the Clock', which told how Bill Haley and his band popularized rock 'n' roll (Shuker, 1994:255). There were disturbances at many screenings as authorities confronted young people dancing in the aisles (Davis, 1990:161). The cinema riots cemented the link between rock 'n' roll and teenagers and they also made it easier to draw one other important association with the new music, namely 'juvenile delinquency' (Bradley, 1990:56). Concern about the behaviour of Teddy boys was not unusual, especially after a notorious murder on Clapham Common in 1953, but the association with rock 'n' roll threatened to cast the entire emergent teen culture in the same light (Davis, 1900:143, 164-165). As Haley gave way to Elvis Presley, concerns about the moral credentials of the new music were heightened. His representation of sexuality in both words and stage demeanor was routinely regarded as scandalous by older people, the height of all that was crude and vulgar (Bradley, 1992:64).

The furore surrounding the emergence of Haley and Presley established a precedent which linked youth music and morally questionable behavior. Although the easy availability of records made rock 'n' roll accessible to diverse social groups, its initial reputation ensured that it was thought fit only for working class youth and 'wayward elements in the grammar schools' (Chambers, 1985:29). For those who rejected it however, opposition was not just a matter of morality but also involved aesthetics.

Musical Fusion

On 20 July 1956, 'Rock Around the Clock' was reviewed by the *Daily Mirror* newspaper. While anticipating its appeal to young people, the review imagined that parents would hear it as 'deluge of discord'. In similar fashion, critics commonly complained that rock 'n' roll was 'not music but a noise' (Chambers, 1985:21). This phenomenon may well have had something to do with the fact that British audiences had not heard music of this nature before. Before the arrival of Haley, Presley and others, America had dominated popular music in the United Kingdom through styles that ranged from show business to jazz, but rock 'n' roll was novel (Chambers, 1985:18). At the same time, there were those who were aware of the origins of rock 'n' roll. One of most frequent abusive comments made of the new sound was that it was 'jungle music' (Bradley, 1992:90-91). The esteemed conductor of the BBC Symphony Orchestra, Sir Malcolm Sargent, for example, suggested that Haley's music was 'Nothing more than an exhibition of primitive tom-tom thumping' (Palmer, 1996:51). Beyond the attempt at ridicule, there was in these kinds of comments a 'racist dislike' of rock 'n' roll's pedigree, a pedigree which was founded on Afro-American musical codes (Bradley, 1992:91).

The music that the early rock 'n' roll stars drew upon and popularised was not the conventional music of white America. It was music that had its ultimate origins in Africa and was brought to America via the slave trade. From the 'rhythm, work songs and field hollers' of slaves there developed spirituals, which in turn provided the source for a whole variety of black music including blues, jazz and gospel (Darden: 2005:1). In the early years of the twentieth century, these came to influence white audiences and jazz especially became popular. But the Depression marked the beginning of a new period of separation between black and white, graphically illustrated by the formation of numerous black urban ghettos. It allowed a period of relative musical isolation in which jazz and blues styles diversified and developed. By the end of the 1940s, there was a wide range of this music available in America (Bradley, 1992:45). From this musical milieu, Haley fused his white country music with an imitation of 'Northern' or 'city' dance-blues which had been popular in the 1940s and 1950s (Bradley, 1992:57), while Presley produced a musical hybrid steeped in country, gospel and the blues (Buskin, 2003:16). The musical fusions established by Haley, Presley and others, created new musical sounds, but they clearly reflected the particular qualities of black music.

Descriptions of the defining characteristics of jazz, blues and gospel invariably focus on a small number of key themes and contrast these with traditional western music. Dick Bradley's work is typical. In a concise summary, he compares the European tradition of music associated with 'classical' and various types of 'light' music, which he labels as 'tonal', and black sounds:

> The rhythmic pattern in general is more prominent than in most tonal-European music, while the *harmonic* parameter is less so, that techniques of vocal production outlawed from most tonal music are prominent, and that extensive improvisation is central in all this music.
>
> (Bradley, 1992:44)

Bradley's summary focuses first on the rhythmic nature of black music. The urban blues bands that emerged during the 1940s and 1950s were renowned for rhythm sections, which provided a strong persistent beat, alongside lead instruments which embellished the music with counter rhythms (Darden, 2005:23). But as Bradley notes, harmonic features were not so important. This is well reflected in Haley's appropriation of black sounds. Although his music was invariably strong on rhythm, inclined to make people want to get up and dance, some of his songs 'were hardly 'tunes' at all' (Bradley, 1992:59). The focus on rhythm and the relegation of melody reversed the typical values of western music. Darden encourages his readers to consider the difference between 'Tea for Two' and 'Oh Happy Day' in order that they might get a sense of the different musical traditions. The accent on the metronomic beat and melody of the former song contrasts strongly with the free rhythms of the latter.

The second of Bradley's defining characteristics of black music concerns vocal presentation. In the western classical tradition, the typical singing voice is usually the product of serious training, in which there is emphasis on such things as breathing, accurate pitch and clarity of diction (Frith, 1983:18). It is often far removed from the natural voice of the performer. In contrast, the black vocal style can be described as 'heightened speech' which gives free reign to 'the cry, groan, gasp, whoop and scream, rather than the merely conversational tone' (Bradley, 1992:134). These features reflect the expressive, emotional use to which the voice is used in black music. They are well reflected in Presley's early songs in which gasps, groans and even inarticulate murmurings indicated strong feelings, and on occasion sexual references, which polite society did not find acceptable. Although the artist may have been influenced by Country and Western traditions, it mostly suggests a borrowing and a debt to the blues (Bradley, 1992:67). The sense of emotion associated with black music leads quite naturally into the third of Bradley's themes. Improvisation and spontaneity arise out of the immediate feelings of the artist. In the African tradition, it is the 'response of the audience, a fellow performer, even the weather' that shape 'the music's beat, tune, texture, tempo, and effect' (Frith, 1983:16). Consequently, there is a fluidity and variability in black music which sets it apart from a great deal of the western musical tradition. Here, the emphasis is upon following precisely the musical score and the composer's intentions, in which very little room is left for harmonic or rhythmic improvisation (Bradley, 1992:33). Bradley's discussion of Presley's version of the Arthur Crudup song 'That's all Right', illustrates how, even at an early stage of his career, the singer was part of a rather different musical outlook. The composer's work is not regarded as sacrosanct and is significantly altered in terms of rhythm and the prominence of the voice (Bradley, 1992:64-66).

The appropriation of black music's distinctive rhythms, vocal styles and improvisations by white performers, would prove to be enormously important in the development of the pop and rock music of the 1960s. But after the initial publicity and success of rock 'n' roll music in the United Kingdom it did not monopolise the British Hit Parade. Successful music continued to be made by Presley and by black American artists like Little Richard, Jerry Lee Lewis and Chuck Berry but not with any great impact. In 1956 for example, in one of the genre's peak years, the best selling rock 'n' roll record was Elvis Presley's 'Hound dog', but it was only tenth in the overall list of best selling records (Chambers, 1985:39). Part of the problem may have been that it was seen as a specifically American sound. Certainly, there were few British artists who could reproduce it effectively. But there was another type of musical fusion which was able to be imitated by young people and was also to have a significant impact on the music of the 1960s.

Skiffle

Skiffle was brought to the attention of the British public by the success of Lonnie Donegan and his version of the song 'Rock Island Line' in 1956. The overlap between classic rock 'n' roll and skiffle meant that some regarded them as synonymous, as the Reverend Brian Bird, one of the few contemporary chroniclers of skiffle, bears witness (Bird, 1958:96). Bird wanted to differentiate between the two types of music and there certainly were differences. Skiffle used acoustic rather than electric guitars and encouraged many young people to become involved in music through the use of simple, sometimes home made instruments, like the tea-chest string bass, comb and paper playing, wash boards and kazoos (Chambers, 1985:45).

This simplicity was undoubtedly part of its appeal; one needed to know only a few guitar chords to play and before long skiffle became a countrywide phenomenon. The *New Musical Express* described it as 'the biggest musical craze Britain has ever known' (Brocken, 2003:73). But the young people who enjoyed skiffle and became involved in skiffle groups tended to be of a rather different type than those who appreciated rock 'n' roll. In reflecting the mainly middle class appropriation of skiffle, George Melly commented that 'It had nothing to say to the Teddy boys' and that it attracted 'gentle creatures of a vaguely left wing affiliations' (Melly, 1970:29). Despite differences of audience and presentation, rock 'n' roll and skiffle were far from being unrelated. Fundamentally, they drew on unconventional American sounds, largely black music, which did not normally feature in the American charts or Hollywood (Chambers, 1985:45). Donegan, who effectively created the template for the British skiffle craze, sang material which was inspired by American folk and blues (Bradley, 1992:62). Chambers' analysis of Donegan's first successful record is instructive. 'Rock Island Line' was a folk song taken from the repertoire of the black singer, Huddie Ledbetter ('Leadbelly'), while on the flipside was 'John Henry', a ballad common to both black and white folk traditions (Chambers, 1985:47). Donegan himself characterized skiffle as 'Folk song with a jazz beat' (Bird, 1958:v). Indeed, skiffle first emerged from within traditional jazz bands during the late 1940s and early 1950s (Bird, 1958:52-53). According to Melly, it originated from the routine of providing a period of light relief in sessions that were otherwise dedicated to serious jazz (Melly, 1970:168-169). Leading instrumentalists would be given a break, during which time the rhythm section would play a lively rendition of American folk and blues. The stress on rhythm so characteristic of the professional skiffle bands and the numerous young enthusiasts who took it up, strongly suggests that it should be regarded as moving in the same musical direction as rock 'n' roll.

The skiffle craze was a fleeting phenomenon and had all but expired by 1958. The significance of this relatively gentle, white appropriation of American folk and blues was not appreciated at the time. In retrospect, it can be seen to have laid the foundation, along with classic rock 'n' roll, for the musical developments of the 1960s. Foremost of its achievements was the encouragement it gave to musical participation, the placing of guitars into teenagers' hands. As skiffle faded, it raised the issue of where young people would go next with their newly acquired musical skills. The answer for some was the burgeoning folk revival, for others it was the energetic pop of beat and blues and eventually rock music.

Beat and Blues

After the emergence of Elvis and skiffle, the British music scene witnessed a number of toned down imitations of rock 'n' roll style, which can be interpreted as attempts to erase its perceived 'wildness' and 'disturbing appeals to the body' (Chambers, 1985:37ff). Cliff Richard's first hit single, 'Move it', released in 1958 was one of the better attempts at imitating genuine rock 'n' roll. But Richard's next really successful single and his first number one, 'Living Doll', indicated that he was concerned to appeal to a wider musical audience than out and out rock 'n' roll would allow (Chambers, 1985:39). He and his band became part of a music scene in which more acceptable developments of Elvis' style were explored. These included ballads, rockabilly/country and instrumentals (Chambers, 1985:40). However, behind a tamed pop scene there was a burgeoning musical amateurism, which followed the rock 'n' roll and skiffle format of drums and guitars. Such bands performed in dance halls, youth clubs and pubs and provided an alternative style of music from that which could be heard in the charts. They presented music with 'a strong, loud beat, some 'intentional' foreground artistry and a strongly speech derived singing style', all of which reflected the influence of the blues. There were thousands of such groups from the late 1950s onwards (Bradley, 1992:75). It culminated in the British 'beat-boom' of 1963-1965 which was triggered by the success of the Beatles.

The Beatles

Skiffle was a key early influence on every member of the Beatles. In 1956, John Lennon and Paul McCartney first performed together as the Quarry Men, a skiffle group (Harry, 2004:14-15). Eventually however, skiffle gave way to rock 'n' roll and their music reflected the influence of Elvis Presley, Little Richard, and especially Buddy Holly. In the August of 1960 they became the Beatles and in less than three years, with the settled line up of Lennon, McCartney, George Harrison and Ringo Starr, they made such an impact upon British youth that the press gave it the name of 'Beatlemania'. In 1963, Beatles' songs occupied the number one spot for eighteen weeks. Beatles' merchandise also sold prolifically. For example, the *Radio Times* printed an exclusive full page picture of the group in September 1963. Copies were available upon receipt of two shillings. A typical response would have been for around ten thousand copies, in the Beatles case, two hundred and fifty thousand were requested (Lewisohn, 2004:64). Most noticeable, was the hysterical reaction of some female fans. At live performances the sound of screaming began to obscure the sound of the music and reduce the amount of time the band performed. The threat of riot ensured that careful thought was given to appropriate performance venues (Lewishohn, 2004:63). Despite the obsessional behaviour of some of their young followers, the reaction of adults to the Beatles' success was largely favorable. There was little of the hostility that marked the entrance of Haley and Presley a few years earlier. This was no more clearly evidenced than in November 1963, when the band played before the Queen as part of the Royal Variety Performance.

The older generation's largely positive reaction to the Beatles can be explained in a number of ways. The Beatles' manager,

Brian Epstein, ensured that they were appropriately packaged for popular appeal. In the first place, this meant exchanging their leather stage gear for suits (Black, 2004:29). But his influence also ensured that any rebellious inclinations, especially on the part of Lennon and Harrison, were controlled (MacDonald, 1998:25-26). It is also the case that the Beatles appeared at a time when there was a great deal of optimism surrounding teenage youth. John Davis' account of societal attitudes towards young people during the twentieth century, suggests a constantly shifting scenario, in which hope and despair alternate and co-exist. But at the turn of the sixth decade, he indicates that the image of the newly emerged teenager was a very positive one and that the Beatles benefited from this:

> At the height of Beatlemania the universally known figures of John, Paul, George and Ringo seemed to define in one way or another most of the positive qualities of the supposed new youth of the late 1950s and early 1960s: energy, wit, lack of time for hypocrisy and pomposity, refusal to bow before the worn-out conventions of class society, etc. In this respect the early image of, and national obsession with, the Beatles can in fact be regarded as an extension of the cult of the teenager.
>
> (Davis, 1990:193)

It is also likely that the nature of the Beatles' music also contributed to their acceptance beyond the confines of youth culture. Certainly, there were aspects of their work that was not likely to win the approval of the older generation. The Beatles were inspired by contemporary black sounds, as well as classic rock 'n' roll and their version of the Isley Brothers song 'Twist and Shout', was particularly thrilling to young audiences. MacDonald's analysis of the song concludes:

> The result is remarkable for its time: raw to a degree unmatched by other white artists – and far too wild to be acceptable to the older generation. As such, it became a symbolic fixture of the

group's act during Beatlemania: the song where parents, however liberal feared to tread.

(MacDonald, 1998:68)

However, although the music of the Beatles might be described as fresh and vital, it was seldom, in the early years, revolutionary. Despite their debt to black music and rock 'n' roll, the songs of Lennon and McCartney also reflected the heritage of western music associated with show business and Broadway (Macdonald, 1998:54, 80). The strong tunes and recognisable melodies, so much a feature of this tradition were an important part of the Beatles' music. McCartney in particular was a gifted melodist. The result was a fusion in which elements of both western music and black sounds were discernable (Chambers, 1985:62). MacDonald's comments are again apposite: 'The Beatles ability to be two contradictory things at once – comfortably safe and exhilaratingly strange – has been displayed by no other pop act' (MacDonald, 1998:94). It was a balancing act which enabled them to earn the approval of a wide audience. Other young musicians, however, were not so concerned about musical balance.

Contradictory Youth

The Rolling Stones, like the Beatles, had an interest in classic rock 'n' roll music, but in their early years they were more concerned to appropriate the urban electric blues of Chicago and contemporary soul music (Chambers, 1985:66). They were part of a blues scene, which had begun to grow following the visit of the electric blues man, Muddy Waters, in 1958. Audiences for early British blues bands were mainly found on the fringes of the folk and jazz worlds, where blues of an acoustic nature was highly regarded by purists. The electric blues tended to be seen as a compromise with pop culture (Bradley, 1992:77). Nevertheless, there developed an intense rivalry between jazz and modern electric blues as to who could provide the most 'authentic' interpretation of black music (Chambers, 1985:69). The popular success of rhythm and blues bands like the Rolling Stones helped to displace jazz from its former prominence. In London, old jazz clubs, like the Marquee and the Flamingo, were transformed into venues featuring rhythm and blues and soul, while the popular music magazine *Melody Maker,* formerly a strong supporter of jazz, was forced to reduce its coverage (Chambers, 1985:70-71). It was at the Flamingo that the Rolling Stones first performed live in January 1963. By the end of the year, after their first album stayed at number one for eleven weeks, and with the success of similar groups, like the Animals, there was an increasing awareness that a new musical phenomenon was emerging. As engaging as it was to certain sections of middle class youth, it did not have the same appeal to parents (Bradley, 1992:78).

In contrast to the Beatles, the Rolling Stones presented as an example of disturbed and deviant youth which did not res-onate with older generations. Their commitment to the blues and its jarring rhythms suggested no hint of western musical traditions that an older audience might relate to. An appro-priation of blues realism, allowed little room for romantic, teen lyrics, which had long been a key characteristic of pop and was occasionally to be found in the Beatles' music. In-stead, with titles like 'The Last Time', 'Get off my Cloud', 'Under my Thumb and 'Stupid Girl', anti-sentimentalism was mixed with strong suggestions of misogyny (Chambers, 1985:68). A preoccupation with male sexuality was also com-municated through the stage presence of their lead singer. In his insider's account of pop history, Simon Napier- Bell com-ments: 'When they saw Mick Jagger's leering manner and swaying hips, they guessed the worst (Napier-Bell, 2002:60). At the same time, it needs to be recognized that just as the Beatles were presented as a picture of wholesome youth, so the Rolling Stones were packaged in exactly the opposite way by their manager, Andrew Oldham. It was he who helped in-stigate and perpetuate the bad boy image, which made them synonymous with 'surliness, squalor, rebellion and menace' (Frith and Horne, 1987:101).

The less than wholesome image of the Rolling Stones may have played a part in the erosion of optimism surrounding the teenager that existed at the start of the decade. By the mid-1960s, images of youth become rather more ambiguous and contradictory (Davis, 1990:186). This is particularly noticeable in the image of the mod. For a period, their seaside conflicts with rockers caught the attention of the country and provoked a moral panic about the nature of young people and the future of the country. The mods, like the Teds, originated in London's outer suburbs, but unlike them, were upwardly mobile, 'often had lower white collar jobs and were 'standard bearers for the working class in an age of affluence' (Osgerby, 1998:42-43). Consumption was very much part of their style and included a passion for blues and soul, scooters, amphetamines and fashion (Frith, 1983:220). They presented themselves as clean, smart and modern. Although the mods were vilified in the press for their skirmishes with the rockers, newspaper supplements presented them as trendsetters for the new Britain in the same breath (Davis, 1990:189). Indeed, the commercialisation of mod style was at the heart of pop fashion and came to be associated with Carnaby Street and 'swinging London'. Whatever was young, new or trendy, became mod (Green, 1999:74). At the heart of this construction was the new music of beat and blues. According to Chambers:

> Around 1964-65 there occurred a decisive shift in the economy of public imagery surrounding pop music. Pop stopped being a spectacular but peripheral event, largely understood to be associated with teenage working class taste, and became the central symbol of fashionable, metropolitan, British culture. It had moved from being a show business mutant to becoming a symbolisation of style.
>
> (Chambers, 1985:57)

The progress of beat and blues, revolving around the figure heads of the Beatles and the Rolling Stones had been astonishing. It was accompanied by the renewal of a rather older style of music.

The Folk Revival

Folk music experienced something of a revival in the years after the Second World War. Behind the boom were organisations like The English Folk and Dance and Song Society and the Worker's Music Association (WMA). The WMA proved to be especially influential, sponsoring the folk journal *Sing*, an independent record label (Topic records), song books and books. The most important of the latter, was undoubtedly A. L. Lloyd's *The Singing Englishman*. First published in 1944 and later republished as *Folk Song in England*, it played a key part in the post-war revival (Brocken, 2003:20). Radio air play was also important. As well as giving space to the music itself, key figures like Lloyd and Ewan MacColl helped produce educational and entertainment programmes (Brocken, 2003:22). For the BBC, folk was a genuine part of British cultural heritage and therefore worthy of support. The institution's conservatively minded leaders may not have warmed to the associations of folk music with left wing politics, but the BBC and the folk movement were united in their intense dislike of American commercial popular music (Brocken, 2003:44). In contrast to what they regarded as the inferiority of this type of product, folk stood for authenticity and truthfulness. Indeed, folk aficionados were often very concerned to capture and preserve what they imagined to be the original folk sound (Boyes, 1993:216ff). This often meant finger-in-ear singers performing unaccompanied or with only prescribed instruments (Brocken, 2003:84). There was a concern to preserve folk music from being contaminated with other musical genres and alien influences. As the post-war boom suggests, this strategy of identifying folk with music that was uniquely British and part of the nation's cultural heritage was not without success. As Britain looked to rebuild after the war, folk music's associations with community, the countryside and an idyllic past, was very attractive (Boyes, 1993:3-4). For some, it was simply the music of the people.

Despite the revival of the post-war years, it has to be said that folk music remained largely marginal to the lives of most young people. For example, the air play that folk music received on the radio took place on the BBC's Home Service or the Third Programme, neither of which were prime sites for young listeners, who preferred Radio Luxembourg (Brocken, 2003:21-23). The irony for folk enthusiasts was that when more young people were touched by folk music, it was not as a result of their concern for musical purity. The musical hybridisation that was skiffle provided the template. The popularity of folk music in the 1960s also came about as a result of a fusing of styles. For a general family audience, there were a number of 'middle of the road', 'variety' artists, who produced music which might be said to approximate to folk, or to have produced a gentle fusion of pop and folk. These included substantial recording artists like Val Doonican, the Bachelors and the Seekers (Brocken, 2003:87, Larkin, 2002a:28-29). None of these would have been regarded as carriers of true folk tradition by the purists. Nevertheless, there can be no doubt that they succeeded in widening the appeal of folk music. But it was the arrival of American folk artists which did most to raise the profile of the music among young people. By far the most significant of these was Bob Dylan.

Bob Dylan

Dylan first became known to British audiences through a version of his song 'Blowin' in the Wind', which was recorded by the American folk trio Peter, Paul and Mary (Larkin, 2002a:184). Under the same management as Dylan, they subsequently released other Dylan songs, and along with the Byrds, helped to promote a pop folk fusion which was influential in its own right. Dylan's own sound was never as sweet; his nasal voice, accompanied by a solitary acoustic guitar and occasional harmonica, presented a very distinctive sound in an era which was dominated by the electric sounds of beat and rhythm and blues. As a teenager he had been inspired by a whole range of music, including the classic rock 'n' roll of Elvis Presley, Chuck Berry and Little Richard (Williamson, 2004:8). But an interest in folk music took a decisive turn when he read the biography of Woody Guthrie. He began to model himself on the gritty folk blues singer who wrote about the poor and dispossessed (Williamson, 2004 19-20). Dylan himself became famous through the writing of highly topical and political songs. His name became synonymous with protest and the civil rights movement in the United States after 'Blowin' in the Wind' became the 'battle hymn' of the movement. His entrance into the British charts in 1965 with 'The Times They Are A-Changin' was strikingly prophetic (Chambers, 1985:86). Along with others like Joan Baez and Barry McGuire, Dylan forged folk as a tool for protest.

Bob Dylan's articulate, highly literary compositions, presented a strong contrast with the 'lyrical simplicities' of much of contemporary pop music (Chambers, 1985:86). Indeed, the combination of compelling lyrics, politics and acoustic style proved to be very alluring for his largely middle class audience. For those who did not insist on folk 'purity' his fusion of folk and blues represented a type of music which was truly authentic. The sense that he was committed to creating serious, insightful, truthful music resonated with young people who were disillusioned with the commercially driven nature of pop. This perception of Dylan was reflected in the words of the British folk singer, Martin Carthy. Carthy had worked with Dylan, and in 1965, wrote an article entitled 'The Dylan I Know' for the Disc Weekly. In a gushing tribute it included the following:

He would never have set out to become a commercial success; he is far too much of a sincere person to do that. There is absolutely nothing 'showbizzy' about him. That he has become popular is purely incidental. He is completely unaffected by his sudden fame. Of course, he has made lots of money from his songs and personal appearances. But this doesn't mean a thing to him. He is just doing what he wants to do.

(Disc Weekly, 10 April 1965:4)

Carthy's assured portrayal of Dylan, as one who is true to his creative instincts and not restricted by commercial considerations, suggests that he knows such qualities will be approved by readers. Similar claims to virtues of self expression and sincerity were part of the appeal of jazz in the 1950s and featured strongly in the philosophy of the beatniks. At the start of the 1960s, these unconventional middle class youth had a significant impact on public consciousness. Inspired by existential philosophy and by the writings of various North American intellectuals like Jack Kerouac, they disengaged from society and cultivated an image of 'studied dishevelment' (Osgerby, 1998:83-84). They lionised creativity and introspection and were deeply attached to jazz, poetry, eastern mysticism and drugs. Although not kindly disposed to conventional politics, they featured very strongly in the support of the Campaign for Nuclear Disarmament (CND). In many ways they prefigured the counter-cultural movements that were to flourish during the second half of the 1960s (Osgerby, 1998:83). Before the arrival of the hippies, but after the peak of media interest in beatniks, Carthy's article indicates that among some quarters of middle class youth, there was a strong attachment to the bohemian values of creativity and self expression and unwillingness to compromise with commercial pop music. This sensibility was undoubtedly a major factor in Dylan's appeal.

The perception of Dylan as a purveyor of authentic music helps to explain the extraordinary reaction which accompanied his decision to go electric. In 1965, he went to the Newport Folk Festival and performed an electric set of songs with the

Paul Butterfield Blues band. Folk purists were appalled. Peter Wicke chronicles the response of Theodore Bikel in the magazine *Broadside*: 'You don't whistle in church and you don't play rock 'n' roll at a folk festival' (Wicke, 1987:102). Undeterred, Dylan went on tour with his new sound. The United Kingdom section proved notorious for walk outs, slow hand claps and cat calls (Sounes, 2002:255-256, Williamson, 2004:68-72). Despite this unpalatable reaction, Dylan had provided a glimpse of the future in which the worlds of folk and electric music would create a new synthesis (Anderson, 2003:235). Towards the end of the decade, groups like Fairport Convention, Steeleye Span and Pentangle helped establish the folk rock genre, while folk inspired sounds fed into the growing progressive rock movement through the likes of Barclay James Harvest and Genesis (Brocken, 2003:96). Indeed, Dylan's electric turn was to be a key factor in the development of rock music.

Rock Music

The distinction that is made between rock and pop music is not straightforward or precise. Commentators have long interpreted the terms in different ways (Frith and Horne, 1987:74). Nevertheless, it is common for historians of popular music to locate the birth of rock music within the latter part of the 1960s (Buskin, 2003:74, Chambers, 1985:84ff, Frith and Horne, 1987:71ff). During this period, themes of authenticity which had previously been associated with folk and jazz became associated with mutated forms of beat and blues. In contrast to pop music, which was thought to be tainted by its pursuit of commercial success, rock was presented as that which focused on the music for its own sake. Indeed, the idea of the rock musician as an artist, who, unshackled by commercial pressures gave full reign to self expression and creativity, was at the heart of the new ideology of rock (Frith and Horne, 1987:56). Such artistic and expressive sensibilities were directed into popular music through a number of important channels. In what follows I will identify three of these streams and indicate how they helped shape the character of rock music.

Dylan and Art School

In his early career, Bob Dylan was resident in Greenwich Village, New York. It was a location which had long been home for writers, musicians and artists. When Dylan arrived in 1961, folk music was highly popular among the literary, bohemian residents, who regarded it as music of integrity and seriousness (Sounes, 2001:101). In many ways his early music and career was the embodiment of artistic ideals that were common among the bohemian society of Greenwich Village. Chief among these was the strongly poetic and literary nature of Dylan's compositions. Whether with his early protest songs or his later elusive compositions, like 'Subterranean Homesick Blues' and 'Like a Rolling Stone', he 'rolled back the horizons of the pop lyric' (MacDonald, 1998:145). His valourising of the word was in marked contrast to the lyrical simplicities of much contemporary pop music (Chambers, 1985:86-87). The Beatles publisher Dick James, for example, complained that their lyrics didn't 'go anywhere' or 'tell a story' (MacDonald, 1998:144). As a result of Dylan's work they began to give more serious attention to words and to reflect his poetic sensibility. Indeed, his departure from acoustic sounds showed that it was possible to combine a lyrical seriousness with an edgy blues style. This expressive concern epitomised the rock music that came to prominence during the second half of the 1960s and was used as a means to differentiate it from pop music. Unusual, quirky and sometimes incomprehensible lyrics became associated with bands like Cream, Pink Floyd and Yes. Although critical of the 'poetry of rock', Frith summarises the convention: 'In rock, words mattered; in pop, it seemed, they did not. Rock verse was poetry; pop verse was mired in the limited language of sentiment, in the rhyming simplicities of moon and June' (Frith, 1983:34-35). Inspired by Dylan's creativity, rock appropriated a literary sensibility through which it announced its claim to be taken seriously as authentic art.

Another creative stream which contributed to the peculiar character of rock music was the British art school. Frith and Horne's book *Art into Pop* has been important in exploring this context for the evolution of rock music (Frith and Horne, 1987). They focus on the art school cultivation of artists who, as creative heroes, are charged with challenging convention by being true to themselves and their art. It was an ideology in which self-expression was prioritised and contrasted sharply with utilitarianism and commercialism (Frith and Horne, 1987:27ff). From the mid-1950s to the mid-1960s, liberal admission policies allowed school leavers with limited academic qualifications, but with 'some sort of creative potential' to enter this world (Frith and Horne, 1987:80). It yielded a large number who went on to achieve success in pop and rock music. Among those who went to art school were some of the most influential musicians of the 1960s and 1970s and included: John Lennon, Keith Richards, Eric Clapton, Pete Townsend, Eric Burden, Ray Davies and Jimmy Page. Through these and others, the bohemian sensibilities of art school were implanted into rock (Frith and Horne, 1987:73). For example, it appears that the emphasis upon self-expression helped to establish a tradition of improvisation and extensive soloing. The group Cream was particularly important in developing this feature. When former art student, Eric Clapton, came together with Ginger Baker and Jack Bruce in 1966, it was to help the former play his 'ancient and modern blues' (Frith and Horne, 1987:89). However, in practice their music went well beyond a strict blues format and the group became famous for their live performances which included long, improvised sections. The heightened sense of expressive individualism that inspired this is reflected in the words of Clapton:

My whole musical attitude has changed. I listen to the same sounds and records with a different ear. I'm no longer trying to play anything but like a white man. The time is overdue when people should play like they are and what colour they are.

(cited in Frith and Horne, 1987:89-90)

The ideal of self-expression, reflected through improvisational soloing, became part of the character of rock music. The guitar hero became especially important. Inspired by Clapton and others like Jimi Hendrix and Jimmy Page of Led Zeppelin, the guitar solo became a prominent feature of the rock genre. Although this was most evident in live performances it also had an impact on studio work. Those who wanted to valourise words and virtuoso soloing found the sub-three minute single increasingly unsatisfactory. The pressure to produce a commercial product was perceived to be a hindrance to the task of creating serious music. Accordingly, the LP format, which allowed much greater space for musical expression became the chosen media for such groups.

Counter-Culture

One other channel of artistic sensibility which helped shape the nature of rock music was the counter-cultural movements associated with the second half of the 1960s. These were an invigoration of beat and beatnik culture which had come to prominence at the end of the 1950s and early 1960s. Its rebirth was due in no small part to the expansion of higher education, which allowed many more middle class young people the opportunity to explore and consider the options it presented (Osgerby, 1998:88). Counter-cultural sensibilities varied quite widely as Osgerby's summary describes:

Focal concerns of the counter-culture were disaffection with (and symbolic disaffiliation from) 'mainstream' society and its institutions, a disenchantment with organized politics, an emphasis on creativity and expressivity and a desire for self-exploration through drugs, mysticism and 'journeys' through dimensions of both geography and consciousness.

(Osgerby, 1998:88)

The most influential of these concerns for the development of rock music was the focus on creativity and expressivity linked with drug use. At the heart of American counter-culture, in San Francisco, there developed a type of music, acid rock or psychedelic pop or rock, which combined sound with light shows, dance, poetry and drugs (Chambers, 1985:89). The idea of such a 'total experience' or 'happening' was thoroughly art world in origin (Frith and Horne, 1987:94ff). It indicated a concern for experimentation and exploration in popular music that was to become an important factor in the development of rock. Its impact in the United Kingdom was most discernable to the general public through the music of the Beatles. In 1967, they released the album *Sgt. Pepper's Lonely Hearts Club Band*, which became a symbol of the new psychedelic trend. 'Fundamentally shaped by LSD' (Lysergic acid diethylamide), the favoured drug of the counter-culture, the album was richly inventive (MacDonald, 1998:220). The band experimented with unorthodox song structures, unconventional sounds and instruments and an array of musical genres (MacDonald, 1998:190ff). Its wide accommodation of different musical styles and song structures would be readily appropriated by those who were prepared to go beyond the pop format. Indeed, at counter-cultural music venues in London, this was already happening:

In venues such as the UFO, the Electric Garden (later named Middle Earth) in Covent Garden, and the Roundhouse in Camden Town, a series of the most startling musical syntheses started to emerge. All shared a sense of experiment, improvisation and free interchange between existing pop and non-pop categories.

(Chambers, 1985:99)

One of the most influential of these new groups was Pink Floyd. They began by playing beat and blues music and appropriated the San Francisco counter-culture interest in performance and sound experiment (Frith and Horne, 1987:96). Their performances were characterized by length, improvisation and highly visual light shows (Larkin, 2002b:335). Quickly tiring of the pop scene, they began to develop complex styles of composition which involved lengthy songs divided into sections, rather like the mini-suites of classical music. It helped herald the arrival of progressive or prog rock music. The fusion of traditional classical styles with electric sounds represented the culmination of late 1960s experimentation. Associated with bands such as Genesis, Emerson, Lake and Palmer and Yes, its appeal to a largely youthful middle class audience reached its peak in the 1970s. It was music which made great claim to seriousness and superior aesthetics. This was achieved by its associations with classical music, high standards of musicianship and by sympathetic music critics, who reviewed LPs with the seriousness normally reserved for the artifacts of high art. However, by majoring on western musical traditions like melody and sequential structure, it tended to lose touch with the Afro-American rhythmic inheritance on which so much of 1960s new music had been built (Chambers, 1987:107ff).

Popularity

The differentiation of rock music from pop arose in a context in which bohemian, artistic values became attached to beat and blues music. A commitment to self-expression, through lyrical seriousness, improvisation and experimentation, though initially associated with avant-garde, artistically minded communities, eventually became part of the underlying philosophy of rock. The irony was that as attempts were made to create authentic music, distinct from the commercial music of the pop charts, it became very popular. A commitment to alternative music, which lionised certain perceptions of creativity and self-expression, could be extraordinarily lucrative. Although middle of the road, easy listening styles continued to be popular throughout the 1960s, the story of the musical revolution is essentially a story of a marginalised type of youth music, (rock 'n' roll), mutating and evolving so as to eventually occupy a central part in the nation's cultural life. By 1969, a revitalised folk music and the emergence of beat, blues, rock and array of different fusions of these, had transformed popular music.

2

Pop Gospel

The success of the Beatles inspired the formation of thousands of beat groups across the country. George Tremlett claimed that in 1963 there were 20,000 groups of this sort in the United Kingdom, including four hundred in Liverpool and six hundred in Newcastle (cited in Bradley, 1992:73). Young Christians were not removed from this extraordinary outburst of musical activity. This chapter will show how Christian beat music was used to attract others to the Christian faith through experimental worship and by direct evangelism. If the typical venue for the former was a church building, the usual venue for the latter was the coffee bar. It will be seen that those who usually used beat music, and later rhythm and blues, as a tool to challenge the unconverted were evangelicals and that they were also the first Christians to appropriate electric music in the service of the gospel. I will demonstrate that the development of Christian pop was dependent upon the work and co-operation of a wide range of people. In the final section, explanations will be offered as to why the Christian pop pioneers have received so little recognition. But first, I examine the emergence of worship with a beat.

'Church with a Beat'

A perusal of the *Church Times* and *Methodist Recorder* for the year 1964 reveals the emergence of what were often described as 'beat services'. These were youth orientated acts of worship in which the musical accompaniment was provided by drums and guitars. In June, the phenomenon even made the front page of the *Methodist Recorder* as the main item of news. The headline 'Church with a beat' told the story of a new style of church, designed 'exclusively for young people' in the village of Hartington, Derbyshire (*Methodist Recorder*, 11 June 1964:1). The brain child of four young people, it met in an appropriately decorated church basement and featured music provided by two electric guitars, a piano, an accordion and drums. The Hartington venture was unusual, in that it was an attempt to create a church specifically for young people using beat music as a major component. More common, were intermittently arranged youth services in which the music would be provided by a beat group or a number of these. During 1964, the *Methodist Recorder* provided numerous examples of this type of event. In May, its youth page commented 'Reports continue to arrive from all over the country of beat or pop services' and offered a guide as to how they might be arranged (*Methodist Recorder*, 14 May 1964:14). Even the *Church Times*, which only rarely commented on issues related to youth culture, published details of beat services. In one article, it reported that the Warriors, a beat group from Accrington, provided some of the music for a special service in Manchester Cathedral (*Church Times*, 10 April 1964:20). While yet another reported that one thousand and seven hundred young people crowded into Christ Church, Birkenhead, for a 'Merseybeat' service (*Church Times*, 20 March 1964:11).

It must also be said, (in the light of social historians like Martin and Segrave, Cloonan and Street's inability to locate secular sources which suggest that Christians engaged in a positive way with 1960s youth music), that there is ample evidence of local newspapers reflecting the emergence of Christian beat and beat services. One of the most popular Christian groups was the Crossbeats, described as 'The Beatles of the Christian beat scene' by Christian beat enthusiast Ed Nadorozny (Nadorozny, 2007). The web site dedicated to their work and ministry reveals a number of newspaper cuttings from their native north-west and beyond. The group was the subject of reports and pictures in their own local newspaper, the *Bootle Times,* on a number of occasions (Crossbeats, 2004a). Their participation in a one day cruise to the Isle of Man, in which they performed on board ship, was reported by the Liverpool *Daily Post* in the August of 1964 (Crossbeats, 2004a). The group's small tour of England in 1965, which included venues in Hereford and Bristol, was reported by newspapers in these areas and included pictures of the band (Crossbeats, 2004a). Local newspapers also drew attention to less well known Christian groups and the experimental worship of which they were a part. In Boston, Lincolnshire, for example, the local newspaper reported on a 'rock service' at the Centenary Methodist Church in the town (*Boston Standard*, 1964:February/March, precise date unknown). Over five hundred people attended the service, which revolved around two local beat groups, the Seminoles and the Fenlanders.

As I will show, many of the Christian groups who performed at beat services did not restrict themselves to experimental acts of worship, but in 1964, their existence was highlighted by the publicity surrounding beat in church. Many Christian beat groups were established during the period of the beat boom. For example, between 1964 and 1971 the Crossbeats came across over forty other Christian groups, most of which would have been within easy driving distance of Liverpool (Crossbeats, 2004a). The Crossbeats' popularity ensured that they performed well outside of this area, in the August of 1970 they even went on a tour of America, but the majority of their work was still located around their native north-west. This suggests that the bands with whom the Crossbeats came into contact were a small percentage of the total number (Crossbeats, 2004a). Inevitably, like their secular counterparts the musical competence of these groups varied considerably. One of the most competent and most well known was the Joy Strings. This Salvation Army beat group came to national prominence as a response of the Army establishment to the new music. They even managed to make the hit parade with the songs 'It's an open secret' (1964) and 'A starry night' (1966). Whilst most Christian groups did not achieve the recognition of the Joy Strings, they did tend to share the same kind of evangelical spirituality.

Evangelicalism

Historians usually locate the origins of Evangelicalism with the evangelical revival of the eighteenth century. Evangelicals themselves often trace their roots back to the Reformation and other important spiritual influences have been Puritanism and Pietism (McGrath, 1994:11ff). It is not to be equated with any particular church and operates across the denominations (Bebbington, 1989:1). In his classic study, *'Evangelicalism in Modern Britain'*, David Bebbington identified four essential characteristics of Evangelicalism as conversionism, activism, biblicism and crucicentrism (Bebbington, 1989:5-17). Conversionism reflects Evangelicalism's concern for a personal encounter with God through which lives are changed. Activism points to a practical emphasis upon mission and service. Bebbington reflects Evangelicalism's respect for the bible by use of the word Biblicism. Finally, crucicentrism indicates the important place that evangelicals have given to the cross of Jesus Christ. All of the themes to which Bebbington refers have helped give a distinctive shape and character to evangelical communities. The stress on conversion and activism has been especially important. It gave to evangelicals an overriding interest in mission and evangelism and a concern to make the gospel relevant to the people of their own times (Ward, 2005:14-16). When applied to music, it persuaded evangelicals that they should use popular forms. In David Martin's essay on Christianity and music he labels this kind of approach 'demotic'. As he says:

> The notion of musical worthiness is pushed to the background. It is not so much a question of 'right' qualities in the music itself,

though one may note a religious potential in this or that piece *en passant*, as its helpfulness in gaining and maintaining assent or conversion. Almost anything will do whatever its origin or style, provided it gets the message across.

(Martin, 2002:49)

The demotic tradition in Evangelicalism is long and noteworthy. The Wesleys, William Booth and Ira Sankey for example, all appropriated secular tunes and styles (Bebbington, 1989: 174, Routley, 1982:42-43, Wilson-Dickson, 1992:185ff). From the 1960s onwards this approach to music came into its own. Evangelicalism responded to the new music of young people far more positively than did any other part of the church.

The Origins of Evangelical Pop

One of the first Christian beat bands was the Pilgrims and aspects of their story offer clues about the initial development of evangelical youth music in the United Kingdom. One of these features suggests that skiffle played a role in providing some early Christian beat musicians with their first experience of playing in a band. Before they became Christians and helped form the Pilgrims, three members of the band had previously belonged to a skiffle group (Derrick Philips, correspondence, member of the Pilgrims, 06 July 2005). The move from skiffle to new forms of electronic music was not unusual and is well attested. Hank Marvin and Jet Harris of the Shadows were former skifflers, as were Lennon and McCartney and a whole host of guitarists who went on to achieve fame in the world of rock music (Chambers, 1985:47, Brocken, 2003:77). It appears that some members of Christian beat groups made a similar musical journey, although the extent to which skiffle played a part in the musical development of Christian beat band members was largely dependent upon age. By 1958, skiffle was a spent force; consequently those young teenagers who began to play the guitar from this period were not likely to find it an attractive proposition. Indeed, if they were at all like the Pilgrims they looked for musical inspiration else where.

When the Pilgrims came together in 1961, until the Beatles became popular in 1963, the group performed songs which reflected the distinctive style of the Shadows (Nadorozny, 2005). In his classic account of modern popular music, Iain Chambers suggests that the Shadows 'probably inspired more British pop beginnings than any other single musical event' (Chambers, 1985:23). One of those beginnings was that of Christian electronic music, most ably represented by Pilgrims. But they were not the only church based group imitating the music of the Shadows or other toned down rock 'n' roll of the era. In Purbrook in Hampshire for example, a beat group called the Renegades was attached to the Methodist youth club. They often performed in secular venues, but they also developed a religious repertoire and participated in special acts of worship in local churches. As the beat-boom developed they came to reflect this style, but they began, in the first years of the 1960s, by imitating the Shadows and other approximations of rock 'n' roll like Adam Faith and Billy Fury (Neil Burnham, interview, member of the Renegades, 30 June 2005). Even if Christian groups did not literally imitate the sounds of the Shadows or other similar artists, they appear to have been important early influences. Certain members of the Crossbeats for example, were influenced by the ballad singing of Paul Anka, the country music of the Everly Brothers and the instrumental guitar style of Duane Eddy (Crossbeats, 2004b). It appears then, that the first electronic music to be appropriated by Christians preceded the influence of the beat boom. However, as the musical journeys of the Pilgrims and the Renegades illustrate, these sounds were quickly left behind as the Beatles became popular. As Eddie Boyes of the Crossbeats observed, 'the real impetus' for the new Christian music 'was the emergence of rough-edged secular groups like those of the early Merseybeat era' (Eddie Boyes, correspondence, 04 July 2005).

Purposeful Beat

Christian beat bands were commonly used to attract young people to the Christian faith. There appear to have been two main strategies to achieve this. One involved an attempt to make worship more relevant to young people; the other approach used beat groups in a form of direct evangelism. Although the latter predated the growth of beat services in 1964 and continued after it declined, the idea of making young people feel comfortable within an act of Christian worship looked back to a tradition before the age of beat music. The 'Twentieth Century Folk Mass' was produced by Father Geoffrey Beaumont in the late 1950s. Beaumont, an Anglican priest, set the service of Holy Communion to what he considered was the people's music. The common abbreviations of this service such as 'Folk mass', 'Jazz Mass' or 'Skiffle Mass' offer an idea of what this was thought to be (Bird, 1958:104). Beaumont devised the service; 'To bridge the gulf between the sacred and the profane' and declared that he wanted people 'to feel at home in the church' (cited in Bird, 1958:107). In the Reverend Brian Bird's account of skiffle, he sympathetically enlarged upon Beaumont's comments:

> To the man in the street, to young people in particular, Church music today is utterly incomprehensible. But it need not remain so. If the people's own music is used in church, the people will come back and sing. And if a skiffle group is hammering out the rhythm at a service, the teenagers may be surprised to find themselves at home in God's house.
>
> (Bird, 1958:109)

The concept that youth music might enable teenagers to 'feel at home' and be integrated into the worshipping life of the church appears to have been part of the reasoning behind the emergence of beat services. One of the ways in which this can be observed is through the recorded statements of those involved in this worship, which commonly stressed the worshipping needs of young people and the legitimacy of youth music. For example, the Methodist minister, Reverend Raymond Brown, was instrumental in organising a beat service in Luton. He commented, 'Young people should be able to worship in their own natural way' and suggested that 'The Church must begin, at some time or other, to learn by trial and error how best to help them' (*Methodist Recorder*, 14 May 1964:14). That Brown's beat service followed in the tradition of the 'Twentieth Century Folk Mass', and the idea of enabling people to feel comfortable in church, is underlined by the fact that it included items from Beaumont's Mass (*Methodist Recorder*, 14 May 1964:14). Again, in the *Methodist Recorder*, the formation of the youth church at Hartington was motivated by the need to present the faith using language and media which were intelligible to young people, something, which according to those who established the new venture, it had singularly failed to do (*Methodist Recorder*, 11 June 1964:1). In an Anglican context, the Reverend Vernon Sproxton, who spoke at the beat service in Manchester Cathedral, was also motivated to help his young audience feel comfortable. As he 'defended modern pop music' he not only supported modern musical tastes but affirmed its place in the church (*Church Times*, 10 April 1964:20).

If one use of beat music was to place it in the context of worship, as a means of integrating young people within the worshipping life of the church, a more common use was in direct evangelism. The two functions were not mutually exclusive, but for evangelicals, the formation of beat bands was strongly linked to the idea of gaining converts. As the Seekers, the Crossbeats began their evangelistic work before the beat service boom of 1964; although they were caught up in this and continued thereafter to perform in church contexts, their primary motivation was clear: 'When we first started, our particular emphasis was on witness and evangelism so that, at that time, playing to a hall full of Christians seemed to us to be 'wrong' (Crossbeats, 2004c). The missionary focus of many of the Christian beat groups was often suggested by their name. With labels like the Heralds, the Witnesses, the Envoys, the Gospel Messengers and the Outreachers, there was little attempt to hide the purpose of their music. Bebbington's theme of evangelical conversionism is well reflected in such groups, their desire to share the Christian faith with their unbelieving contemporaries was paramount. Consequently, bands like the Crossbeats eventually played in a wide array of venues including night clubs, beat clubs, colleges, concert halls, prisons, but above all they performed in coffee bars.

The Coffee Bar

The coffee bar became an important part of teen experience during the 1950s and 1960s. Before pubs and discotheques became attractive places to congregate, coffee bars provided a place where young people could meet, chat and listen or dance to music. They represented freedom from parental over-sight and, as entry was inexpensive, at a price they could afford (Osgerby, 1998:41). The most famous coffee bars were in London but in most provincial towns it was possible to find a network of espresso bars and 'dives'. It was upon this cultural phenomenon that evangelicals fashioned their 'coffee bar evangelism' and with which Christian beat groups became strongly associated.

The first Christian coffee bars which featured beat music opened during 1963 and 1964 and quickly became the major way in which evangelicals attempted to attract young people to the Christian faith. In the autumn of 1967 for example, seventy per cent of the Crossbeats' performances took place in coffee bars (Crossbeats, 2004d). In comparison, the number of beat services, which first announced the arrival of the Christian beat bands to a wider constituency, declined. This is explicit in the kind of bookings that the Crossbeats accepted. Meticulous record keeping allows it to be seen that in 1964 the group had over thirty church based bookings, four years later they performed at only two (Crossbeats, 2004a). The use of beat music as an evangelistic tool clearly appears to have triumphed over the idea that it could be used to integrate young people within the worshipping life of the church. A number of reasons can be adduced for this. Eddie Boyes, a former member of the Crossbeats, raised the twin possibility that on the one hand churches might have been less inclined to offer invitations to beat groups, while at the same time, beat groups were less inclined to accept them (Eddie Boyes, correspondence, 28 March 2007). The reluctance of churches to continue with beat services might indicate congregational disquiet, but there might have been other reasons, including the practical difficulties of creating youth friendly worship around beat bands. Organising regular events, when bands, as the Crossbeats' web site shows, were in great demand, was not easy, nor was the effort involved in setting things up. Roger Hurrell, an evangelical who performed folk music from the early 1960s, contrasted the flexibility of his sound with that of the Christian electric groups: 'You didn't have to lug big amps around! So long as the PA was ok you could 'play and go' (Roger Hurrell, correspondence, 09 July 2005). The reluctance of beat groups to perform in churches probably reflected their evangelistic priorities. Secular venues and appearances at coffee bars appeared to be a more effective way of sharing the gospel than performing in an act of worship.

Coffee bars provided a relaxed atmosphere where Christian young people could invite their unbelieving friends without fear or embarrassment. They were patterned after their secular counterparts, which included naming the venue in an attractive way. Christian coffee bars had names such as the Lighthouse, the Vine, the Mustard Seed and the Fish. One of the most well known was the Catacombs in Manchester. A typical visit to a Christian coffee bar would involve live performances, conversation and coffee against the backdrop of piped music. Provision was also made for an evangelistic speaker to address the young people (Crossbeats, 2004d). The combination of popular music, personal contact and public address appears, judging by their popularity, to have worked well for a period. But by the start of the 1970s, the perceptive were beginning to realize that coffee bars were no longer the most effective ways of sharing faith with young people. In January 1970 for example, the evangelical youth magazine *Buzz,* discussed the future of coffee bars with the heading 'Coffee bars-RIP' (*Buzz,* January 1970:6). Most of those who contributed to the article were not quite so ready to accept that verdict. But the truth was that young people were gravitating to other venues and the coffee bar as a national phenomenon was on the decline. Nevertheless, 'Coffee bar evangelism' was one of the most potent illustrations of Evangelicalism's use of pop music as a tool of outreach to young people.

The Message

The lyrics of the songs that evangelical beat bands performed were uncompromising and challenging. In a straightforward manner they focused upon the Christian faith and the need to embrace it. This often meant that lyrics involved a direct challenge to turn to God. Of the sixty three self penned songs to be found on the Crossbeats' website for example, nearly half (thirty), are of this character (Crossbeats, 2004e). In the early stages of writing their own material, appeals to believe centred on the biblical drama of creation and redemption. But this was quickly superseded by an attempt to explain how God might improve ones life, through an experience of love, meaning or satisfaction. A typical example of this recourse to the subjective benefits of faith is the song 'Something's Missin'', written in 1964:

> You may think you've got everything.
> You may think you don't need a thing.
> And go on living by yourself
> Well, listen, something's missin'

You go to parties all of the time.
You may think that you're doin' fine
Is this your life from day to day?
Well, listen, something's missin'

There's something missin' and Jesus is His name
Although you're sinful, He loves you just the same
Why not take Him right away, and let Him come in to stay
He'll be your Friend right from the start
Well, listen, something's missin'.

(Millington, 1964)

Some of the Crossbeats' songs reflected the cultural and social developments of the 1960s. In 1965 for example, they produced one of their most popular songs 'Crazy mixed up generation', which refers to protest singers and beatniks. But as the climax of the song illustrates, the Crossbeats were more concerned with evangelism than social comment. The problems of the world become an opportunity to declare the individuals need of Jesus:

Let's face it friends, the world is in such a mess
Before life ends, let's start livin'
Kid's that live for kicks know no way to fill the emptiness
Protest songs are hits, but what 'they sayin'
They say that we're lost, we're all sittin' waitin' for the bang
We know that we're lost, but what's the answer?

Crazy mixed up generation, there is only one solution
Jesus is the Great sensation
Won't you stop and think, now you're on the brink?

Beats think life's a joke, these long-haired cynics of society
They don't do a stroke, but why should they?
Mum and dad at home have lost control of their pride and joy.
Oh how they moan 'What's the answer?'

Can you be so blind, you can't see the truth about yourself?
Or don't you mind where you're going'?
Jesus knows it all; He knows your situation now
Why do you stall when he's the Answer.

(Boyes and Knowles, 1965)

The lyrical content of Christian beat group songs could not be described as sophisticated or impressive, poetically, but they suited the purpose for which they were designed, which was to directly challenge young people about their need of Jesus Christ.

Supporting the Beat

The emergence of Christian beat was dependent upon a wider constituency of Christian support. In what follows a number of these sources of assistance are identified.

'Trendy Vicars'

The use of beat bands in church worship inevitably suggests that such events received the support of local church leaders and clergy. The *Church Times* and the *Methodist Recorder* of the period reflect this theme. In reporting a 'Merseybeat' service at Birkenhead for example, the *Church Times* drew attention to the involvement of the vicar, the Reverend L. R. Skipper. Skipper not only arranged the service, but also authored one of the new hymns which the beat group performed (*Church Times*, 20 March 1964:11). As this example illustrates, clergy were frequently involved in beat services as organisers, leaders of worship and as speakers, but the initiative for such experimental worship did not always begin with them. The *Methodist Recorder* highlighted on a number of occasions that beat services arose out of the enthusiasm of young people themselves (*Methodist Recorder*, 27 February 1964:3, 14 May 1964:14, 11 June 1964:1). The production of the music was largely left to youth. In the May of 1964 the *Methodist Recorder's* youth page featured a story about a beat service in which a minister had helped by adding his voice to the singing group (*Methodist Recorder*, 14 May 1964:14). That this was headline news suggests that it was not common and the accounts of beat services in the *Church Times* and the *Recorder* support this view. The image of the trendy, guitar wielding vicar, as presented by Dominic Sandbrook does not appear here (Sandbrook, 2006:433, 439). Nevertheless, clergy played an important supportive role in the emergence of Christian beat music and perhaps this is best illustrated by the willingness of some to acquire chaplaincy roles. The Crossbeats were attached to St Leonards, a lively evangelical Anglican Church in Bootle, Liverpool. The curate, the Reverend John Banner, was not only their manager and secretary but also their 'spiritual advisor' (Crossbeats, 2004f). Clergy could even exercise a spiritual role to secular beat bands. In 1965, the *Methodist Recorder* reported that the Reverend Brian Brown had become chaplain to sixteen beat groups, including the successful Merseybeats, which were managed by the McKiernan Theatrical Agency (*Methodist Recorder*, 13 May 1965:18).

Hierarchy

The most obvious example of church assistance at an institutional level was the Salvation Army's involvement in founding and organising the Joy Strings. The group began almost by accident. In 1963, the new leader of the Army, General Frederick Coutts, was asked in a radio interview about the Christian faith and young people, he responded by saying that if the Army had to play electric guitars to reach them, it would do so. The national press seized on this comment and the media wanted to see photographs of the Salvationists using this new sound (Boons, 2005). Consequently, the Army felt bound to act. Captain Joy Webb, who was on the staff of the Army's International Training College in London, was identified as someone who possessed the appropriate qualities and the venture grew from there. Within a very short period came television appearances, a hit single and touring.

The formation and ministry of the Joy Strings was extraordinary in being so closely linked to the hierarchy of a church. The benefits of this might be described as mixed. On the one hand, the band was able to draw on the resources of the Army, which meant among other things, that the Joy Strings' recordings were of a high quality (Ed Nadorozny, 2007). On the debit side, the control of the Army was absolute, which meant that even the groups continuing existence was dependent upon the leadership. The initial end point for the group was to have been the summer of 1965, this was extended, and in fact they didn't finish until 1969. But this decision was regarded as premature by some, not the least of whom was the Joy Strings' bass player, Bill Davidson, who thought that they were at the height of their popularity and effectiveness. He argued that the decision was based on other matters:

> The Salvation Army really had a hard time dealing with such enormous popularity involving some of its young officers….. and some within the organisation had always resented what they felt was 'special treatment' for members of the group …..which was bogus! The HQ decided it was time to move on…..which, for them, meant 'move back."
>
> (cited in Ed Nadorozny, 2007)

Perhaps it was natural for Davidson to feel upset by the Army's decision to end the group. But the nature of its control over the Joy Strings project meant that the decision to conclude or continue was always going to be theirs, and given its progressive nature, there was always the possibility that the group might be finished on issues unrelated to evangelistic effectiveness. What is significant for this study, however, it that these unrelated issues, according to Davidson, did not appear to include opposition to beat music. He points to concerns about the high profile of the Joy Strings' members as being decisive factors in the decision to finish the group. Moreover, the ending of the Joy Strings does not support the suggestion of those who have argued that the church was singularly opposed to beat music and its use in the church. The Salvation Army may have chosen to bring the group to an end at an inopportune moment, but by this time it had already supported them for five years, and through them had shown that Christians could enjoy beat music and use it in the service of the gospel.

Musical Gospel Outreach

In December 1964, a number of gospel groups met in West Ealing, London, to share experiences and to discuss difficulties. From this initial conference, Musical Gospel Outreach (MGO) was formed the following year (Ward, 2005:28). In the years that followed, MGO was to be at the forefront of the development of contemporary evangelical music in the United Kingdom. It arranged concerts and tours, published song books, established Key, its own record label and through its magazine, *Buzz*, simultaneously reported and publicised the burgeoning youth culture of Evangelicalism (Ward, 2005:30, 45-46). It was founded however, with a more limited remit. This focused on the need to help Christian musicians. Ward quotes Pete Meadows, one of those involved in the establishment of the organisation: 'MGO was there to train and equip those using music to share their faith' (Ward, 1996:90). One of the ways that it did this was through the organisation of conferences. The growing size of the evangelical music scene can be observed by the fact that around three hundred musicians regularly attended MGO's annual get together during the latter part of the 1960s (Ed Nadorozny, interview with Geoff Shearn, former MGO leader, correspondence, 03 April 2007). Another way in which MGO supported evangelical musicians was through the publication of *Buzz* magazine. This first became available in October 1965 and consisted of eight sides of A5 paper (Crossbeats, 2004g). In this early period, it offered information about Christian bands along with help and advice for those starting out along this route.

One of the most important things that *Buzz* provided was the words and music of songs written by established Christian beat bands. It reflected one of the key areas of difficulty for all new Christian groups, the lack of specifically Christian beat songs. At the early beat services, the bands tended to adopt a number of musical strategies: they might play beat versions of traditional hymns and songs, put modern tunes to traditional words or use contemporary songs, which although not overtly religious, had a spiritual dimension. The *Church Times* report of a youth service at Manchester Cathedral, which featured the Warriors beat group, reflected each of these approaches. The Warriors led the congregation in a beat version of 'All things bright and beautiful', performed another familiar hymn, 'Father, hear the prayer we offer', to the theme tune of the television series *Z Cars*, and also used Bob Dylan's 'non-religious pop song' 'Blowin' in the wind' (*Church Times*, 10 April 1964:20). These strategies reflected the fact that there was little these groups could draw upon which combined a modern lyric with a modern sound. As was noted earlier, the Crossbeats wrote many of their own songs, but initially they too faced this difficulty and performed modern hymns and American gospel songs (Crossbeats, 2004e). It was far from being an ideal situation, and the Crossbeats, along with other pioneering groups began to produce their own material. This was not an easy task, especially when one considers that performing a large number of ones own songs was a recent innovation of the Beatles, and not every Christian group had the ability to do this. Consequently, the publication of words and music of modern songs in *Buzz* magazine went some way in helping to provide new groups with appropriate material. In more general terms, the support of MGO in providing advice and training, clearly contributed to the competence of evangelical musicians and ultimately to the growth of contemporary Christian music in Great Britain.

The People

Whatever help MGO might afford, it is clear that most Christian beat groups relied upon the goodwill and support of local Christian people. One of the most remarkable examples of this was the endeavor that surrounded the music of the Crossbeats. The support that the group received from the ministerial leadership team of St Leonards, Bootle, was only the tip of a very large iceberg. A number of people were involved in getting the group bookings. Individuals provided transport, help with equipment and even stage suits. The group also had three hundred 'prayer partners' who would pray for the band, (Crossbeats, 2004h). Crucially, the Crossbeats were also fortunate to have a musical advisor. Tom Cooper was the organist, choirmaster and lay reader at St Leonard's and 'probably the most important Christian music influence on the Crossbeats' (Crossbeats, 2004i). In the early years, before the band began to write their own material, it was he who supplied the band with songs and helped with musical arrangements. The extent of the Crossbeats' support may have been unusually large, but getting a beat band 'on the road' was not a simple matter. It usually demanded the collaboration of a number of other people. It suggests that alongside the many Christian beat bands that appeared in the 1960s, there were also teams of Christian supporters who were in sympathy with what they were trying to do.

Beyond Beat

Christians were not slow to take hold of the new beat music and to use it in worship and evangelism. It also appears they could be rather slow in laying it down as other pop music became more popular. Christian beat music continued to be used by evangelicals in their outreach initiatives throughout the 1960s. The Crossbeats continued with their form of beat music evangelism well into the 1970s (Crossbeats, 2004b). However, there were those who were prepared to venture out and adopt a different approach. Drawing more deeply on the blues, bands appeared that played rhythm and blues. Like their secular counterparts these groups tended to stretch pop sensibilities to their limit and stood on the verge of rock style.

Despite indications of resistance to musical change, the emergence of Christian rhythm and blues was, at least in part, a story about moving on from beat. Some of the Christian rhythm and blues bands and some of the artists who performed in them had previously played in a beat style. One of the latter, was Nigel Robson, who was part of a rhythm and blues band called Calvery Links; he had formerly been a member of the Joy Strings (Ed Nadorozny, correspondence, 03 April 2007). Paul De Barr, a guitarist with The Vigils beat group, relates how it disbanded and reformed as Time and Space, this time with a guitarist who modelled his style on Jimmy Hendrix (Crossbeats, 2004j). One of the most interesting examples of the move from beat to rhythm and blues was that of the Pilgrims. As was observed earlier, they began their career by reflecting the music of the Shadows, during the beat boom they appropriated this sound and then from around the middle of the 1960s, as their rhythm guitarist put it, they began playing 'Rolling Stones style' (Nadorozny, 2005). According to the band's vocalist, Tony Goodman, who was instrumental in forging this new direction, they were the only Christian group playing this kind of music at the time (Tony Goodman, correspondence, 01 August 2005). It is difficult to prove or disprove this assertion, but at a time when beat music was still very popular in Christian circles, there cannot have been many groups who were playing rhythm and blues in 1965. Within the next two or three years, numbers were to increase and it becomes possible to make some comparisons between these groups and the earlier beat bands.

The emergence of Christian rhythm and blues was not of the same scale as the outburst of musical amateurism which marked the birth of Christian beat. The number of rhythm and blues groups was much smaller. Nor was there any attempt to integrate rhythm and blues into the worshipping life of the church. It also seems likely that rhythm and blues groups received less understanding from the church than beat groups. Geoff Shearn, guitarist with the Envoys rhythm and blues band, maintained that the antipathy of the church encouraged them to explore secular venues (Ed Nadorozny, interview with Geoff Shearn, correspondence, 03 April 2007). The same theme is developed by Derrick Phillips, vocalist and guitarist with the Pilgrims, who suggested that 'unwelcoming' churches were a factor in the band's decision to move away from church settings (Derrick Phillips, correspondence, 06 July 2005). Bearing in mind the reputation of certain rhythm and blues bands and the edgier musical style, it is perhaps not surprising that there was hostility. But even here, church opposition to what some of their young members were doing can be exaggerated. Derrick Phillips for example, maintained that it was only a 'few' who were antagonistic (Derrick Phillips, correspondence, 06 July 2005). Nevertheless, it was enough to encourage bands to explore other venues. Although rhythm and blues groups still performed in coffee bars, there appears to have been a greater willingness to play in unconventional arenas. The Envoys for example, involved themselves in 'cold canvassing secular rock venues' in order that they might play during intervals, and also played in pubs, clubs and discos (Ed Nadorozny, interview with Geoff Shearn, correspondence, 03 April 2007). This practice highlights the common ground that Christian rhythm and blues bands shared with the beat groups, namely a passionate desire to share their faith. The lyrics to the songs that the rhythm and blues groups performed were as direct as those of the beat bands.

Forgotten Pioneers

Christian groups like the Pilgrims and the Crossbeats were pioneers, the first to combine electronic music with Christianity. Yet it is surprising how little recognition the beat groups have received. In Tony Jasper's wide ranging discussion of Christianity and youth music, *Jesus and the Christian in a Pop Culture* for example, there is no mention of how young British Christians first engaged with pop music. The impression is given that nothing happened in terms of Christian appropriation of youth styles before 1970. However, there is material which focuses on young Christian artists from America and their influence on Christians in the United Kingdom (Jasper, 1984:96ff). More recently, Pete Ward's accounts of evangelical sub-culture do find a place for the beat bands and especially their role in coffee bar evangelism (Ward, 1996: 89-90, 2005:28-30). But there is little acknowledgment of their role as pioneers. Instead, the emphasis tends to be upon how Christian musicians from America brought 'new life' into British churches attempts to relate to youth culture (Ward, 1996:86-87). Ward's books, *Growing up Evangelical* and *Selling Worship*, each have a chapter devoted to the theme (1996:80ff, 2005:35ff). Important as the American influence was, the space allocated to it tends to reduce the significance of earlier, indigenous musical initiatives. Such studies encourage the common view that contemporary Christian music was born in the United States of America, with artists like Love Song and Larry Norman, rather than with British groups like the Pilgrims and the Crossbeats. The reasons for the low profile of the British groups might include the following:

(1) Christian beat existed before the formation of an effective Christian music industry, which meant that artists found it very difficult to record and promote their music. The infrastructure to support the new music did not exist. The Crossbeats for example, had many offers to record from different Christian record companies: 'But all had assumed that a recording could be done by simply placing a microphone in front of the group in a church – what the Christian labels had been used to doing with choirs' (Crossbeats, 2004k). The Crossbeats eventually persuaded their record company to use secular recording studios which were properly

equipped. The lack of quality Christian recording facilities and, as the Crossbeats' experience shows, an appreciation that they were needed, along with the cost of hiring secular studios, meant that relatively few Christian groups were professionally recorded. Such was the dearth of recorded Christian music that at the Catacombs coffee bar in Manchester, live groups would be recorded and the result then placed on tapes for use as background music at a later point (Crossbeats, 2004d). The emergence of MGO during the beat era was significant and was to play an important role in promoting Christian music in the future, but at this early stage it did not have the capability to enable Christian beat to make a wide impact.

(2) Poor recording facilities obviously did not help artists to present their music in the best way and this may have encouraged the perception that the quality of Christian beat was second rate. In 1979, the Christian author Malcolm Doney claimed that it was 'mostly dreadful' (cited in Scott, 2005:122). Given the outburst of musical amateurism, both Christian and secular, which followed the emergence of the Beatles, that some lacked musical excellence is hardly surprising. The difficulty with a comment like Doney's however, is that all Christian beat music easily becomes associated with the word 'dreadful'. In recent years, the new availability of Christian beat music, both on compact disc and on the World Wide Web, has shown that this was most certainly not the case. But even if it were all of a poor quality, it is questionable whether the first attempts to integrate faith with electric youth music should be ignored.

(3) Christian beat in the United Kingdom lacked a charismatic figurehead. The later growth in the popularity of Christian rock music in the United Kingdom was aided by the exceptional personality of the American, Larry Norman, often described as 'the father of Christian rock'. The Christian beat scene lacked someone with that kind of magnetic personality.

(4) The perspective from America, which has by far the biggest contemporary Christian music scene and the most influence, has tended to overlook the contribution of little known British artists. Authoritative works like Powell's massive *Encyclopedia of Contemporary Christian Music* for example, written and published in the USA, though available world wide, serve to under-line the significance of the early American artists. The British pioneers of the early 1960s on the other hand, receive no mention at all.

There is no doubt that the contribution of the early British beat pioneers has been over-looked in accounts of the development of contemporary Christian music by secular and faith authorities alike. Social historians such as Martin and Segrave, Cloonan and Street, have been culpable for ignoring the Christian beat boom and for suggesting that the church only opposed the youth music of the era. This oversight is matched by Christian commentators who have over-looked the pioneering contribution of the British beat bands.

3

The Turn to Folk

The emergence of Bob Dylan and other folk stylists ensured that whatever popularity folk music had enjoyed in the post war period, it reached new heights from 1965 onwards. It became an important part of the youth music scene. The indications are that the church responded more favourably to this sound than to any other type of youth music. At various points, this chapter will indicate why it did so, its main concern however; will be to demonstrate folk's popularity, largely through the uses to which it was put. But also, initially, through the growth in the number of Christians who performed folk music.

Folk Singers

The Methodist Association of Youth Clubs (MAYC) was founded in 1945 and was one of the most important ways in which the Methodist Church served and interacted with young people. One of the special features of MAYC was the 'London Weekend', a yearly event in which large numbers of young people gathered for conference, worship and entertainment. The latter was provided by a variety show held in the Royal Albert Hall in which items were contributed by the young people. At the beginning of the 1960s the musical component of the display was not especially prominent. In 1961 for example, it included a choir of four hundred young voices, a 'rhythm group', an accordion player and a special guest appearance of the pop star Cliff Richard. These were easily outnumbered by an array of sports finals and dramatic items (*Methodist Recorder*, 01 June 1961:12). There was no item which reflected folk style. By 1964 things had changed. The *Methodist Recorder* reviewer reflected: 'No-one could complain that the show did not have enough music with guitars' (Motson, *Methodist Recorder*, 04 June 1964:14). Beat music and folk music were both well featured. By 1966, the trend towards a greater number of musical items reached its zenith, largely as a result of the inclusion of five different folk groups (*Methodist Recorder*, 19 May 1966:16). There were complaints that the show was being overwhelmed by music (*Methodist Recorder*, 30 June 1966:18). Consequently, the organisers introduced a dedicated music event outside the show in 1967. It only featured one style of music. The 'Folk Festival' offered a two hour programme in which ten groups and individual singers displayed their talents. It received a sympathetic review in the *Recorder*. It was a performance of 'high calibre and a healthy symptom of Methodist youth' (*Methodist Recorder*, 18 May 1967:5). Such an approving comment and the astonishing rise of folk within MAYC illustrated the growing appeal of this musical style within a mainline denomination.

Methodist youth were, according to one of its ministers, a broad coalition of the 'indifferent', the 'thoughtful' socially aware and evangelicals (Dixon, *Methodist Recorder*, 19 January 1967:14). The latter, along with evangelicals from other denominations, were increasingly attracted to folk music. The appeal of folk itself was not a new phenomenon, evangelical folk groups and singers were in evidence from the beginning of the 1960s. Roger Hurrell for example, who was part of the trio Roger, Jan and Michael and then the duo Roger and Jan, turned to folk performance after a London concert featuring Peter, Paul and Mary in 1961 (Roger Hurrell, correspondence, 09 July 2005). As the Crossbeats' web site testifies, folk groups would sometimes appear alongside Christian beat groups during the beat boom period (Crossbeats, 2004a). In early 1964, the *Christian Herald* featured a series in which a Baptist minister, Bryan Gilbert, guided readers on the virtues of using the acoustic guitar and how to begin to play it (*Christian Herald*, 04 January 1964:1). Gilbert had established a 'folk style' group which began in the late 1950s and continued into the beat era (Derrick Phillips, correspondence 06 July 2005). However, these early indications of the appropriation of folk style were as nothing compared to its prominence later in the decade, as can be seen for example, in the content of some of the first LP records released by Musical Gospel Outreach.

The first LP record on the new Key label became available in 1968. It featured an example of 'contemporary folk', courtesy of the Forerunners, a nine piece group from America (*Forerunners*, 1968:sleeve notes). The second and seventh releases were compilations featuring a number of different artists and in many ways, these highlight the character of the evangelical youth music scene at the end of the 1960s and the beginning of the 1970s. *Alive* was released in 1969 and included the work of four groups. Rhythm and blues was represented by the band All Things New, the remaining three, Whispers of Truth, Roger and Jan and the Glorylanders, played folk (*Alive*, 1969). *Alive* was a product of the recording studio, the other record compilation, released the following year, was a live event, part of the *Sound Vision in Concert* tour (*Sound Vision in Concert*, 1970). On this occasion, three out of the five artists, Judy Mackenzie, Carol, John and Aubrey and Trinity Folk, featured folk sounds. The importance of folk music within Evangelicalism is clearly visible through these LP records and was further encouraged by the Jesus Movement.

The Jesus Movement was the result of a Christian revival among the hippie culture of West Coast America during the late 1960s. Thousands of young people became Christians. Among those who were converted were musicians, who then made Christian music in the contemporary styles that they enjoyed (Kendrick with Price, 2002:26, Ward, 2005:36ff). The Jesus Movement produced a wide variety of contemporary sounds, from hard rock through to gentle folk, which came to be known as Jesus music (Powell, 2002:1071). The links between American and British evangelicals ensured that it was not long before the influence of the Jesus Movement was felt across the other side of the Atlantic (Kendrick with Price, 2002:26, Ward:2005:43ff). The musical impact of the Jesus Movement in the United Kingdom undoubtedly helped the development of Christian rock music, especially through the example of Larry Norman. But it also raised the profile of modern folk styles. Mark Allan Powell, who produced the *Encyclopedia of Contemporary Christian Music,* suggested that folk music was one of the favoured musical genres of the Jesus Movement (Powell, 2002:1071). A good case could be made for saying that it was the most favoured style. Many of the names associated with the Jesus Movement, such as All Saved Freak Band, Barry McGuire, Honeytree, Karen Lafferty, Love Song, Phil Keeaggy and Randy Matthews, all used modern folk style to some extent; while Norman performed protest songs in a style evocative of Bob Dylan (Powell, 2002:632ff). In the United Kingdom, where young evangelicals were fascinated by the Jesus Movement and especially its music, the prominent place given to folk styles was significant (Ward, 2005:44) It confirmed the value of folk as a cool, youth oriented medium, through which the Christian gospel could be communicated and celebrated.

Encouraged by the Jesus Movement musicians, the profile of modern folk styles within British Evangelicalism during the early 1970s was extremely high. The number of evangelical artists who were playing some form of folk music was considerable. In Ken Scott's book *Archivist,* he lists and describes the Jesus music that was recorded onto LP during the period 1965-1980 (Scott, 2003). His work offers a comprehensive account of recorded material. Many entries concern artists from the United States of America but music from the United Kingdom is well represented. Scott managed to locate eighty five albums from British artists which reflected some type of folk music. This compares with forty albums of rock or pop music from the same period. The bias towards folk is also seen in the artists who performed at the Greenbelt festival, the show case for contemporary Christian music. The festival began in 1974 and in the early years, folk music was prominent. For example, in its second year it had a dedicated folk tent (Henderson, 1983:16-17). This was in addition to the many folk style artists, like Parchment (formerly the Trinity Folk), Water into Wine, Malcolm and Alwyn and Garth Hewitt, who made it onto the main stage. In 1975, folk music styles varied. Groups like Mask and John and Brian would have been perfectly at home in a folk club environment (Henderson, 1985:6, 7). But those who became well known within the evangelical sub-culture tended to reflect wider youth musical trends and produced various types of folk fusion.

The Uses of Folk

The proliferation of folk performers illustrates how popular folk music became in Christian circles from the middle of the 1960s onwards. Its significance is further underlined by the uses to which it was put. In what follows, I will show how modern folk was used in outreach and worship. First of all however, I consider the place of Christian folk music in communicating social and political concern.

(1) Protest

There was an established link between folk and protest. The leaders of the post war folk revival like Bert Lloyd and Ewan MacColl were committed socialists and stressed what they saw as the genre's innate oppositional characteristics. The growth of the Campaign for Nuclear Disarmament (CND) during the late 1950s and early 1960s was especially important in making folk synonymous with protest (Boyes, 1993:214, 324). Neverthe-less, the early songs of Bob Dylan were fundamental in alerting large numbers of 1960s youth to concerns about civil rights, racism, nuclear weapons and militarism. His early work inspired a whole genre of songs with a message. In 1965, a front page piece in the *Melody Maker* drew attention to this with the headline 'Pop protest songs soar' (*Melody Maker*, 11 September 1965:1). For those Christians who believed that faith implied a concern about the whole of life, including social and political matters, it made folk music an extremely attractive proposition. As Peter D. Smith, a Methodist Minister and editor of the popular *Faith, Folk and Clarity* folk song book explained, folk music was 'an excellent medium for expressing Christian faith and concern' because of its 'association with many of the great religious and humanitarian movements' (Smith, 1967: Preface). In the following I will focus on two examples of how Christians combined folk and protest. One of these will be concerned with the content of Christian folk song books and will major on Smith's collection, but first I draw attention to the use of folk music in special concerts and religious services.

(a) Specials

One of the most interesting accounts of the churches use of folk music to provoke thought about issues of justice is to be found in the Dean of Liverpool Cathedral, Edward Patey's description of a special Christmas service that took place in the Cathedral in 1968. This is how he described the finale of the televised event:

> At this point a young Liverpool folk singer shouted 'stop' and against a filmed background depicting war, famine, homelessness and racial intolerance, sang:
> 'Since He came the world seems the same
> Why on earth did he come?
> What on earth was the Saviour's game?
> Why on earth did he come?

And the commentary elaborated on this dark side of Christmas. Like millions of others, God's son was born a refugee.

Like millions of others, he was a victim of cruelty and injustice.
The broadcast finished on a note of dedication and prayer. First
the whole assembly swinging to *If I had a Hammer*, leading on
to the quiet ending, with a young man standing alone on the
nave bridge speaking the St Francis prayer.

> 'Lord make us instruments of your peace
> Where there is hatred, let us love.'
> (Patey, New Christian, 08 February 1968:4)

Not only was folk music integral to the service but it played a
vital part in communicating its essential message. As Patey's
description shows, folk music was used to raise the question
about the purpose of Christ's coming and was one of the channels, through the singing of *If I had a Hammer,* by which the
congregation was encouraged to respond to the reasons that
were given for it. The *Methodist Recorder* offers evidence of
similar occasions when folk was used to challenge audiences
about human need. One of these also took place in Liverpool.
In 1967, a concert entitled 'Hungry Folk' was organised by
Methodists and Anglicans and held at the Methodist Central
Hall (*Methodist Recorder*, 19 January 1967:14). The
programme of folk music had the practical purpose of raising
funds for the United Nations 'Youth Against Hunger'
campaign. But there was also another important aspect. The
Recorder reported that the concert was 'designed to stimulate
thought on the right of all people to be free from hunger, disease,
poverty and ignorance' (*Methodist Recorder*, 19 January
1967:14). During the second half of the 1960s, Christian Aid,
an agency of the churches concern for the poorest peoples of the
world, organised a number of similar specials. But the most high
profile event which linked folk music and Christian Aid was a
song competition based around the theme of human need. Some
of the winning entries were sung at a special event held at Trafalgar Square in London during 1969. The theme song for 'Songs
from the Square' was Sydney Carter's 'When I needed a Neigh-

bour' and the event was televised as part of the religious series *Hallelujah* (Christian Aid, 1970:endpiece).

(b) Song books

The popularity of folk song books illustrated the high regard that many Christians had for folksong during the second half of the 1960s. As previously mentioned, *Faith, Folk and Clarity* was one of the most popular. Peter D. Smith's collection was meant to be 'only a minor contribution' to the Christian folk scene, but it became 'something of a best seller almost over night' (Smith, *Methodist Recorder*, 06 March 1969:17). It sold so well that Smith went on to edit *Faith, Folk and Nativity*, *Faith, Folk and Festivity*, as well as other folk collections. Some local churches, like the Methodist Church at Notting Hill, prepared their own books which were also very popular. *Songs from Notting Hill* was followed by *More Songs from Notting Hill* owing to the 'great demand' for the songs (Notting Hill Group Ministry, 1972:Foreward). The content of these books shows how the church used the medium of folk music to express concern about social and political matters. Because of its popularity, the focus will fall upon *Faith, Folk and Clarity*.

Faith, Folk and Clarity was published in 1967 and included Mediaeval carols, Negro spirituals, works by folk legends like Woody Guthrie and Pete Seeger, as well as more recent contributions by Christian writers like Geoffrey Ainger and Sydney Carter. It was divided equally between 'songs of faith and worship' and 'songs of freedom and concern' (Smith, 1967:Contents). The first half of the book expressed a good deal that reflected a fairly conventional Christian spirituality, expressed through the idiom of folk music. The second half of the book however, was much more radical. It covered a wide variety of social and political issues such as racial prejudice, freedom of speech, peace and the nuclear threat, poverty and homelessness, drug addiction, the imperative of Christian action and the real possibility of change. What is remarkable about many of the songs in this half of the collection is the direct way in which they address their subject. Jim and Brenda's Stringfellow's song, 'Fair Shares for All' is a good example:

> Let's share the food, my brother,
> Let's share the fruits of the earth.
> Steak for me and rice for you,
> Eggs for me and rice for you,
> It's nice for me, but rice for you;
> Fruit and wine and milk and jam,
> Cheese and pickles and fish and ham
> For me;
> And a little rice, just a little rice
> (If you're lucky) for you.
>
> Let's share the pain, my brother,
> You shall have more than your share.
> Pains for you and pills for me,
> Germs for you and jabs for me'
> Though you die young, long life for me;
> Tranquilisers, deep X-ray,
> Penicillin, and nothing to pay,
> For me;
> And a little clinic, just a mobile clinic
> (Per hundred thousand people) for you.
>
> Let's share the world, my brother,
> Apartheid means equal shares.
> Your land for us, and mine for me,
> Sand for you, and soil for me,
> What's left for you, the best for me;
> Schools and bridges, roads and trains,
> Oil and tractors, libraries, 'planes,
> For me;
> And a nice reserve, yes, a nice reserve
> (When your working life is over) for you.

Let's share the war, my brother,
Let's share the horrors of war.
Peace for me, napalm for you,
Trade for me, but raids for you,
Away for me, at home for you;
Cripples, orphans, refugees,
Villages burned, no leaves on trees,
For you;
And a little pang of conscience, just a little twinge
(Not very often) for me.

Let's share our wealth, my brother,
Let's share all that you have.
Gold for me, and beads for you,
Christ for me, the devil take you;
There's two for me, and none for you;
Bingo, bombs, and drugs, and booze,
Money to burn and waste and lose
For me;
And a little aid, just a little aid
(When we can spare it), for you.

(Stringfellow and Stringfellow, 1967:31)

Apart from its savage critique, this song, like many others in the second half of Smith's collection, is extraordinary by its expression of social concern without recourse to an explicit Christian theology or a specifically Christian argument. As powerful as the Stringfellow's song is, there is nothing that marks it out as being a specifically Christian song. Many of the 'songs of freedom and concern' had a universalism which meant they could be performed by all those who wanted to see reform. By including these types of songs in an overtly Christian collection, it appears that Smith wanted to identify Christian social and political concern with much of the counter-culture agenda, which was then abroad in the western world. There were limits to this identification; *Faith, Folk and*

Charity' did not affirm experimentation with sex or drugs for example. But in style and content Smith's work suggests a very real affinity with some of the youth movements of the period.

In terms of its explicit and potent political message, there can be few popular Christian song books to compare with the *'Faith, Folk'* series. They are one of the most pertinent reminders of how in turning to folk music, Christians reflected something of the counter- culture ethos of the 1960s and joined their voices with those young people who wanted to see the world changed for the better.

Evangelical Protest

A preoccupation with changing social and political realities was not characteristic of evangelicals during the 1960s. They tended to be concerned with issues of personal morality. As Bebbington reports, this was to change in the following decades, but concern with economics and politics was still in its infancy at this point (Bebbington, 1989:264). During this period, it remained the case that 'The widest enthusiasm for public campaigns, as in the nineteenth century, appeared when the target, in evangelical eyes, was sin' (Bebbington, 1989:265). This was most clearly evident in the Festival of Light campaigns of 1971 and 1972 which were concerned with sexual morality. These reveal that when evangelicals turned to protest they also turned to folk music.

The Festival of Light was the initiative of a Baptist mission-ary, Peter Hill, who was concerned about the amount of sexu-ally explicit material in the arts and the media. Among those who supported the campaign against 'moral pollution' were Malcolm Muggeridge, Lord Longford and Mary Whitehouse (Ward, 2005:44). The aim was to reform the Obscene Publica-tions Act (1959), so as to make it a more effective instrument in maintaining public decency (Green, 1999:348). The culmi-nation, on 25 September 1971, was a rally in Trafalgar Square, followed by a march to Hyde Park. In the following year, a similar event was organised with events throughout London and a rally in Hyde Park. In both campaigns, but especially in 1972, music had a significant place. Among the artists who appeared in this year were Cliff Richard and Larry Norman. As previously mentioned, the latter frequently turned to a folk blues sound and it was examples of modern folk, represented by Graham Kendrick, Gordon Giltrap and Roger and Jan that predominated. Most importantly, the unofficial theme song for the event was 'Light up the fire' by the folk group Parchment. Released as a single, it became a minor hit in the BBC music chart (Ward, 2005:45). 'Light up the fire' was not easily recognisable as a song of protest. In fact, it was more of a call to Christians to share their faith than a criticism of the moral climate. Indeed, there is a suspicion that many of those who attended the Festival of Light were persuaded that the answer to the nation's moral decline was more likely to be remedied by evangelism than by legislation (Bebbington, 1989:265). If this idea was reflected in Parchment's theme song, it was also reflected in the artists chosen to perform at the event. Apart from the notable exception of Norman, who could produce scathing lyrics on a par with Bob Dylan, those who performed at the Festival of Light were not known for their protest songs. In terms of addressing the permissive society and the issues that the Festival of Light was supposed to be about, evangelical folk music at this stage in its development was clearly not up to the task. Nevertheless, the key thing to note is that despite its lack of protest songs, when evangelicals wanted music to accompany a national campaign for change, it was largely to modern folk music that they turned.

The closest evangelicals came to producing a quality folk singer with protest songs was Garth Hewitt. In the 1970s, he appeared as a singer/song writer very much in the Dylan mould. He was in fact an Anglican clergyman, and although he sang gospel songs, he also produced songs of social comment and critique. Inspired by Martin Luther King and the musicians connected to the civil rights movement, he felt that social issues were an integral part of the gospel (Hewitt, correspondence, 24 September 2005). Hewitt went on to become a leading evangelical social campaigner and has used his music to draw attention to the plight of the world's poor. During his long career he has used a wide variety of musical styles, but in the early 1970s it was folk that was to the fore, usually combined with rock and country elements (Hollandsworth, 2005). During this period, his concern for social justice was still developing. Nevertheless, he was still capable of writing an extremely challenging lyric. As the song 'The people of the West (Amos rides again)' illustrates:

> You've silenced your prophets,
> You've shot down your dreamers,
> Your life-blood is money,
> You're exploiting the poor.

> Oh the people of the West,
> They just love to invest,
> In the system that keeps the poor
> man poor.

> You have no compassion,
> Your lifestyle is evil,
> Higher living standard,
> That's the God you adore.

> You let justice roll on like a river,
> Truth like an ever flowing stream,
> Then tears of rage will turn to laughter
> And people become what they should be.

> You ignore the ways of justice,
> Though you talk a lot about it,
> You victimise the stranger
> Seeking refuge in your land.

> Greed is your mother,
> Silence is your father,
> Your epitaph is written
> In frustrated tears of rage.
>
> (Hewitt, 1973)

His third album, *Love Song for the Earth*, released in 1976, did not contain anything so outspoken. But it did include a song which addressed the issue of hedonism. 'Live for now' was a song which told the story of an individual, who at the behest of an anonymous 'they', is persuaded to live for the moment. The song suggested that this entailed a loss of hope and meaning which the Christian faith could provide. Hewitt's main problem with the idea of living for 'the thrill of each moment' was the inevitable transitory nature of the experience:

> Bobbie tried to live for the moment
> He tried to live for one day at a time
> But as he lived for the thrill of each moment
> The trouble was the present tense soon got left behind
>
> Live for now, that's what they told him,
> The present experience it's the only thing worth while
> Live for now, that's what they told him,
> But as soon as you're there, the present's left behind.
>
> (Hewitt, 1976)

That Hewitt should choose to criticise the idea of living for the moment is not without significance. As Ian MacDonald pointed out in his celebrated work on the Beatles, the notion of 'nowness', of immediately seeking to satisfy one's passions and desires was central to the 1960s mind set (MacDonald, 1998:18-19). MacDonald argued that this attitude was a genuine break with the careful prudence of the post-war generation and a direct challenge to Christian attitudes, which, he maintained, were focused on the hereafter, rather than the existential present (MacDonald, 1998:18). The extent to which the latter is true is a matter of debate, but there is little doubt that MacDonald's general assertion that the new emphasis upon immediate pleasure and satisfaction did cause the church problems. Christian ideas of restraint and self sacrifice did not always sit very comfortably with a generation determined to live fully for the moment. Consequently, Hewitt addressed this important issue, seeking to expose the limitations and essential meaninglessness of living only for now.

The music of Hewitt and the particular concerns of the Festival of Light earlier in the decade, show a similar disenchantment with the direction that society was taking. It reveals that the association of folk music and protest, so typical of the 1960s, was not lost on Evangelicals. There may not have been a great deal of evangelical protest music, but when they wanted to express concern, modern folk was seen as an appropriate musical medium to use.

(2) Outreach

If protest was not Evangelicalism's forte, their use of folk music as a means of challenging people with the message about Jesus was extensive. However, as I will demonstrate, there were developments which differentiated it from the evangelistic style of Christian beat. But before I turn to Evangelicalism and folk style evangelism, it is important to appreciate that the wider church was also ready to use this style of music to commend the good news. It appears to have done so, largely out of a concern to communicate the relevance of faith.

(a) Relevance

Edward H. Patey's description of the experimental Christmas service held in Liverpool Cathedral contains, what amounts to, an apologia for this special event (Patey, *New Christian*, 08 February 1968:4). The service was a multi-media experience, including dancing, drama, video footage and music. Pop music was provided by the Bee Gees pop group, but there were more examples of folk style. As well as the two folk items at the climax of the service already mentioned, there were folk songs from The Settlers. In the face of criticism, Patey argued that the worship of the church had become too 'churchy', 'imprisoned in a middle class culture' and consequentially 'unable to communicate to the vast mass of people today' (Patey, *New Christian*, 08 February 1968:4). In many ways, he appeared to be echoing the concerns of Geoffrey Beaumont, Brian Bird and those who had advocated the use of beat in Christian worship. Indeed, in practical terms there appears to be little difference between their stress on enabling people 'to feel at home in the church' and Patey's evident desire for a means of relevant communication which would 'speak easily' of the Christmas story to those who would 'not be held' by traditional formats (Patey, *New Christian*, 08 February 1968:4). The music that was best placed to help achieve this was of course, rather different than that imagined previously. Given the content of Patey's service, it was not jazz, skiffle or even pop sounds, but modern folk music which was thought most suited for the task of making faith appear relevant to those outside the church.

The idea of using folk music as a means of making the Christians faith appear relevant is found elsewhere. It featured particularly prominently in a 1969 edition of the *Methodist Recorder*. In May, its youth page ran the headline 'Songs for today's world' and related to two featured items (*Methodist Recorder*, 01 May 1969:16). One of these advertised a forthcoming BBC television production entitled *A Most Peculiar Man* which was an unusual telling of the life of Christ. It interspersed narrative by the Reverend Doctor John Vincent from Rochdale with the modern folk music of Paul Simon. Songs such as 'Sounds of Silence', 'I am a rock' and 'Richard Cory' were to be used to help communicate the message. Alongside this news, the other article appears to act as an apologia for it. Written by Peter D. Smith, editor of *Faith, Folk and Charity*, it rehearsed a familiar theme. The Churches music, vocabulary, architecture and organisation was so often 'immersed in the past that it has little meaning today and hence makes no impact on the present generation' (Smith, *Methodist Recorder*, 01. May 1968:16). The remedy, at least in part, was to turn to folk. The reasons for this did not just concern folk's popularity but also its character. Its ability to express simple faith, challenge, and articulate the concerns of the world, made folk music an ideal medium through which it could be demonstrated that Christianity was 'not merely of historic importance', but was also 'relevant for today's world' (Smith, *Methodist Recorder*, 01 May 1969:16). For Smith, folk songs were the 'Songs for today's world' and if the church wished to commend itself and its message as forward looking and modern it needed to use these type of songs.

Not all of those who used folk music were happy with using it as a means to appear relevant to those outside the church. The music group at Notting Hill Methodist Church which produced a number of popular folk song books was forthright in its criticism. At the end piece of their first collection they declared that the songs 'represent no attempt to be 'with it' or to 'get outsiders in' or any such illicit thing' (Notting Hill Music Group, 1965:end piece). This could be interpreted as a Christian insistence that faith should not be a matter of wanting, or appearing to be popular, but of being true to conviction. Including the idea, that commending faith was about service and behaviour, rather than a matter of relying on tools like music. On the other hand, it could also be seen as an echo of folk ideology, which, as I mentioned in chapter one, lionised self expression and was suspicious of popularity and commercial success. It is not made clear which of these alternatives was in mind. An emphasis upon the fact that the songs were the result of their own 'expression' and that they were written for themselves with no other end in view, perhaps makes the latter interpretation more likely (Notting Hill Music Group, 1965:end piece). Whatever, they clearly hoped that others would follow their example in being true to themselves rather than being concerned about relevance. The evidence above suggests that it was advice that was not well heeded.

(b) Creative Evangelism

Evangelicals had no such qualms about relevance. They were, after all, so profoundly convinced of the relevance of their faith, that they were happy to use trendy beat music as a means of challenging the unconverted. Evangelicalism's use of folk also tended to move in this direction. But as was suggested above, they did not merely replicate the evangelistic strategies of the Christian beat bands. Whilst retaining a challenging agenda, evangelical folk music tended to be rather more subtle and less confrontational than their beat forbears.

At the heart of this change seems to have been a similar kind of folk sensibility which may have caused the Notting Hill musicians to renounce relevance. This was the notion of the folk performer as a creative artist, seriously dedicated to their art and to self expression. For evangelicals who appropriated this idea, it meant that unlike some of the members of Christian beat bands, they did not see themselves as evangelists with guitars but performers with a message. It can be observed in the career of Graham Kendrick. Kendrick was one of the significant figures within the evangelical folk scene during the late 1960s and early 1970s and went on to become a celebrated writer of modern worship songs. As an interpreter of modern folk, he listed his main influences as Simon and Garfunkel, Al Stewart, Cat Stevens, Gordon Giltrap and John Martin; he clearly considered himself, like them, first and foremost a performing artist (Kendrick with Price, 2001:23, 66). That this was how evangelical folk performers tended to see themselves is supported by the songs they sang. A typical repertoire consisted of a great deal more than calls to follow Jesus. Important evangelical artists like Parchment, Malcolm and Alwyn and Garth Hewitt for example, recorded and performed songs which had no explicit Christian content at all. That this was not just a characteristic of the evangelical musical elite is affirmed by my own memories of hearing local evangelical folk music during my teenage years in Lincolnshire. Traditional folk songs or more recent secular pieces would accompany songs of faith.

Perhaps the most potent illustration of what being an evangelical folk performer meant for the presentation of the gospel was to be found in the lyrical content of songs. Christian beat group lyrics could be extremely simple expressions of the need to become a Christian disciple. Evangelical folk revealed a rather more sophisticated style which reflected the influence of Bob Dylan and other folk artists (Kendrick with Price, 2001:23). The perception of folk as a word serious medium could be very appealing. In the case of Graham Kendrick for example, it was the reason he turned to folk music in the first place (Kendrick with Price, 2001:23). He developed a story-telling approach in which he would tell parts of the gospel story from the point of view of one of those involved. Consequently, some of Kendrick's songs have titles like 'The Executioner', 'Nicodemus' and 'Peter at the Breaking of the Bread', while a song like 'Kingdom Come' concerns the reflections of an imagined beggar. He found this 'a good device for getting people to think about who Jesus was' and highlighted the challenge of faith (Kendrick with Price, 2001:34).

The influence of modern folk music's stress on words can also be observed in the work of Malcolm and Alwyn. The duo was one of the most popular performers within the contemporary Christian music scene during the early 1970s. Their sweet harmonies were reminiscent of Simon and Garfunkel and it is no surprise to find that they are listed as one of their main influences on the sleeve of their first album. They also credit Lennon and McCartney and Bob Dylan as sources of inspiration (Wild/Wall, 1973:sleeve notes). One characteristic of their lyrical style was the testimony song. A good example of this is the title track from their first album, 'Fool's Wisdom':

Got myself some wisdom from a leather backed book,
Got myself a saviour when I took a second look.
Opened up the pages and what did I find,
A black and white portrait of a king who's a friend of mine.
Funny how when you think you're right everybody else must be
wrong,
'Til someone with fools wisdom somehow comes along.
His voice was strange and the words he said I didn't quite under-
stand,
Yet I knew that he was speaking right by the leather backed book in
his hand.

Hey, hey, what a day,
Fools wisdom.
Hey, hey, what a day,
Fools wisdom.

Got myself some wisdom from a leather backed book,
Got myself a saviour when I took a second look.

(Wild and Wall, 1973)

Malcolm and Alwyn wrote a large number of such testimony
songs. Of the ten songs on their second album for example,
only three, ('Spaceman', 'Wildwall' and 'England Goodbye')
could not be said to be of this type (Wild/Wall, 1974:tracks
3, 9 and 10). Through personal accounts of spiritually trans-
forming experiences Malcolm and Alwyn invite the listener to
experience the same.

In many ways, there was nothing unusual about Malcolm
and Alwyn's creative way of communicating the vitality of the
Christian faith. Many traditional hymns, including many by
Charles Wesley, majored on testimony (Hempton, 2005:70).
Yet, it is seems likely, that more is reflected here than a modern
adoption of an old theme. As was mentioned in the first chapter, one element within the revolutionary counter-cultural
movements of the 1960s was an emphasis on personal trans-

formation. According to Michael Brocken, by the 1970s this motif was penetrating the world of folk music and signifying a move away from its traditional political concerns (Brocken, 2003:110-11). It is possible that Malcolm and Alwyn and Kendrick (with his gospel story telling), were reflecting this change. Indeed, there is a very particular reason to connect the latter with this new style of folk. Of the five artists that Brocken associates with this move towards introspection, Kendrick names three, Cat Stevens, John Martyn and Al Stewart, as among his key influences, (Kendrick with Price, 2001:23).

Evangelicalism's turn to folk represented some significant changes in how its musicians perceived themselves; the idea of performance took on a greater importance. This in turn affected how they presented their message. The appeal of folk was its word seriousness which encouraged the development of story telling and testimony songs. Moreover, the stress on personal transformation suggested that they were in tune with wider sensibilities within society and within the folk movement.

(3) Worship

The turn to folk which we have observed in the churches outreach and in its concern for the world, was also to have a significant impact upon its worship. Indeed, there is little doubt that the evangelical use of folk in this context proved to be the most long lasting and influential Christian appropriation of youth music; bringing to birth the praise and worship song. But it was the wider church which first considered the merits of using folk style in connection with public worship.

Supplement Songs

Between 1961 and 1969, representatives of the Church of Scotland, the Congregational Church and the Episcopal Church, formed the Dunblane Consultation on Music. Meeting in the small Perthshire town, they examined the state of contemporary church music and were charged with finding a form of musical expression which was suitable for modern times (Fraser, 1985:171ff). Very early on the group was expressing an interest in the relevance of folk music and it was to Sydney Carter that they turned when they wanted to explore its potential (Frazer, 1985:173, 76-177).

Carter was one of the most significant figures in the traditional churches appropriation of folk. His first, definitive encounter with folksong came in Greece during the Second World War. He subsequently immersed himself in the world of folk and dance that was focused on the London Headquarters of the English Folk Dance and Song Society (Williams, *The Independent*, 17 March 2004). Eventually, he edited the Society's journal, *English, Dance and Song* and featured in the debate between folk purists and those who were open to outside influences. Carter was very much on the side of those who wanted to contemporise folk (Brocken, 2003: 48-49). As a writer and a performer, he became acquainted with many of the contemporary artists from the folk scene and his readiness to explore new folk frontiers can be seen in their diversity, colleagues included both Rolf Harris and Maddy Prior (Williams, 2004:2). It was this open type of folk music that Carter sought to commend to the church. In the 1960s, he produced many songs which were widely sung, including 'Judas and Mary, 'When I needed a Neighbour' and his most famous creation, 'Lord of the Dance'. In tune with the world, many of Carter's songs reflected the theme of protest. As hymnologist and secretary of the Dunblane group, Eric Routley, later noted, 'Lord of the Dance' criticised traditional church immobility and 'When I Needed a Neighbour' implied that the church was not a neighbour to those in need (Routley, 1982:81). Nevertheless, Routley was happy to affirm Carter's work. This was not without significance, given that he favoured 'very solid, serviceable, and dignified' liturgical music (Routley, 1964:Preface). In 1964, before Carter was well known, he announced that his use of satire and irony within a religious context was 'remarkable' (Routley, 1964:184). He clearly felt that Carter's songs, with their challenging lyrics, could make a contribution to Christian worship. Routley's verdict was clearly shared by the Dunblane Consultation on Music, which declared 'Folk is a root from which contemporary things can grow' and used Carter's compositions in their song supplements (Fraser, 1985:177). The group produced a number of these and they were at the leading edge of church discussions about hymnody and modern music. They set an agenda that others were to follow, both in the production of supplements and in their willingness to appropriate folk music.

By the middle of the 1970s, most of the main denominations in Great Britain had followed the example of the Dunblane group and produced supplementary volumes to their hymn books. Within a few weeks of each other in 1969, the Anglicans brought out *100 Hundred Hymns for Today* (Proprietors of Hymns Ancient and Modern, 1969) and the Methodists published *Hymns and Songs* (Methodist Church, 1969). In 1974, the Baptists produced *Praise for Today*, while The United Reformed Church followed with *New Church Praise* the next year (Routley, 1982:94). A good deal of this material was in the main stream of the British hymn writing tradition. There was a stress on using appropriate language for modern times and the volumes exposed the work of new hymn writers such as F. Pratt Green, Brian Wren, Fred Kaan and Timothy Dudley Smith (Routley, 1982:95). But they also allowed space for more innovative developments in which folk style had a prominent position.

The Methodist supplement contained seventy four hymns in a more or less conventional style and twenty five songs. The preface acknowledged that the latter were of a largely experimental nature and questioned whether they might find a permanent place in Christian worship. At the same time, it suggested that these 'new creative impulses ought to be received with sympathy' (Methodist Church, 1969:Preface). Although categorisation is an imprecise science, based on the descriptions provided (such as for example, 'Negro Spiritual'), arrangements (such as the inclusion of guitar chords) and authorship, it is possible to see that many of the experimental songs had their roots in the folk tradition. Five of the twenty five songs reflect folk traditions from around the world: 'Jesus the Lord Said', 'Let us Break Bread Together', 'Our Father', 'Were You there?' and 'What Wondrous Love'. At least another eight, can be regarded as expressive of a native folk idiom: 'Black is the Earth', 'Mary's Child', 'Every Star Shall Sing a Carol', 'Lord of the Dance', 'The Advent Ring', 'Judas and Mary', 'When I Needed a Neighbour' and 'Christ in Need'. In total, thirteen songs, around a half of the compositions in the songs section of *Hymns and Songs*, can be said to reflect a folk style.

Theological Challenges

Hymns and Songs was prepared for publication during the second half of the 1960s, the folk component in the songs section, reflected its popularity and the sense that it was appropriate for use in worship during this period. It is likely that one reason for this was the ability of folk song to challenge and provoke, as Routley had mentioned in connection with Carter's work. *Hymns and Songs* included a number of such songs, including Carter's 'When I Needed a Neighbour'. Yet, other pieces in the folk idiom, like 'Let us Break Bread Together' and 'Jesus the Lord said' expressed a more conventional personal devotion. These twin themes of sustaining faith and unsettling it are echoed in other folk collections of the period, including *Faith, Folk and Clarity* and the Notting Hill books. In an article entitled 'Folk in Church Worship', Carter also brought these themes together. Unsurprisingly, he favoured the idea that folk music in church should encourage 'self-examination', but he also acknowledged that 'singing something securely Christian to a folksy melody .....may do some good' (Carter, *New Christian,* 18 April 1968:9). These sentiments, and the contents of the supplements and song books, suggest that it was upon these two virtues, that the growing sense that folk music could be used in Christian worship was based (Smith, *Methodist Recorder*, 01 May 1969:16).

Those folk songs which expressed the dimension of challenge were usually related to the theme of Christian living and the need to express faith in terms of a concern for justice and peace. As has already been noted, this allowed the church to connect itself with the counter-cultural movements of the period. However, Christian theology could provide the motivation for a social concern. The field was dominated by the Bishop of Woolwich, Dr John Robinson's book, *Honest to God* (Hastings, 2001:536). Published in 1963, the Bishop's work provoked much debate and sold nearly a million copies in three years. His stress on what he called 'worldly holiness' was one of the more uncontroversial aspects of his radical theology (Robinson, 1963:84ff). Its appeal to a spirituality which embraced the whole of life and engaged with the secular was widely practiced. This is best illustrated by the variety of new Christian social initiatives during the 1960s, which included Shelter, the Cyrenians, Cicely's Saunder's Hospices and Amnesty (Hastings, 2001:543). Post-war developments, like Christian Aid, the Samaritans and the Cheshire Homes also flourished during the decade. Christians were motivated to take their worldly responsibilities seriously and folk songs echoed to such themes. The radicalism more directly associated with the Bishop, such as his preference for divine immanence and a new morality based on love was not so well represented. However, there were songs that reflected Robinson's discussion of the incarnation. The Bishop was reluctant to use the term and rejected traditional interpretations because of a concern that they denied Jesus full humanity (Robinson, 1963:65-66). In tune with Robinson's anxiety, folk writers produced material which stressed the humanity of Jesus. Geoffrey Ainger's song, 'Christ in need' for example, depicted a Christ who was not an all sufficient saviour figure (Ainger,

1969:99). He needed the help of others to fulfill his ministry; even the culmination of his work was dependent on human aid. Christ was presented as a very human person. One of the most thought provoking applications of this theme was by Sydney Carter. In the song 'Son of man', he used the title to refer to Jesus humanity and contrasted it with the term 'Son of God', which spoke of his divinity. The second and third verses created very different scenarios:

> But if I were the Son of God,
> And if they crucified me,
> I'd think I was luckier
> Than those who hung beside me.
> I'd know that I would rise again,
> And all things would be well,
> But when you are a son of man
> However can you tell?

> If you are a son of man
> Then you can be mistaken;
> You hang upon a cross of doubt,
> You feel you are forsaken.
> And whether you will rise again
> Is more than you can tell;
> And if you were the son of man
> You've tasted that as well.
>
> (Carter, 1967:10)

The piece allowed the person of Christ to identify with human doubts and struggles, but for those who were not used to such applications of Jesus' humanity, Carter's lyrics were of an unsettling nature. Despite the work of Ainger and Carter, echoes of controversial debates within the church were not common in folk songs. The main way in which they tended to provoke was through the need to take social and political realities seriously.

Worship Songs

If the evangelical appropriation of modern types of folk music can be illustrated by the way it was used in protest and evangelism; it was its use of folk styles in worship that was to be the most far reaching. In helping to create an entirely new genre of Christian music, the influence of evangelical folk was to affect many churches far outside the evangelical constituency. This section briefly describes the growth of charismatic spirituality, from where the new worship songs originated and goes on to explore their character, through one of the most important, early collections of songs, *Sound of Living Waters*.

The charismatic renewal movement was essentially an appropriation of traditional Pentecostalism by those within the traditional churches. At its centre was an experience of being 'baptised in the Holy Spirit' through which lives could be dramatically changed. Moreover, the gift of the Spirit was associated with the ability to speak in an unlearned language (speaking in tongues), spiritual gifts and miraculous healing (Rosman, 2003:288). Although the movement touched a wide variety of Christians, including Roman Catholics, most charismatics were evangelicals (Rosman, 2003:289). Chief among these was Michael Harper. A curate at All Souls, Langham Place, in 1963 he resigned to establish the Fountain Trust, an organisation established to promote charismatic renewal within the established churches. Through its magazine *Renewal*, it encouraged those who had been baptised in the Spirit to remain within their existing churches (Bebbington, 1989:230). On the whole, this advice proved remarkably successful, but the tension between charismatic and non-charismatic sometimes proved intolerable. Charismatics who felt unwelcome in their usual place of worship, often joined what were initially called 'House churches', then Restorationism and still later New churches (Bebbington, 1989:230, Brierley, 2000:39ff). These churches pre-dated the renewal movement, (Bebbington dates them from 1958), and usually had their roots in the independent, Free Church tradition (Steven, 1989:3). They were generally anti-denominational by conviction and desired to restore the pattern of church life found in the New Testament (Bebbington, 1989:230). Nevertheless, the similarity of charismatic renewal and Restoration in terms of worshipping styles and songs, made it easy for former members of traditional denominations to move (Ward: 2005:41). By the start of the new millennium, the growth rate of charismatic churches had begun to slow. But something of their dramatic rise can be seen by the fact that from small beginnings in the early 1960s, charismatics were the largest grouping within the evangelical movement by 1989 (Brierley, 200:54).

The success of charismatic Christianity has been attributed, in part, to its convergence with contemporary cultural developments (Bebbington, 1989:233, Rosman, 2003:292). Significantly, large numbers of charismatics were young people and as it emerged in the 1960s, it appeared to be 'a Christianised version of the new youth culture of the day' (Rosman, 2003:292). Bebbington draws attention to a number of characteristics that charismatic Christianity shared with 1960s counter-culture (Bebbington, 1989:240ff). Among these characteristics were self expression and creativity, and these helped to bring about an explosion of new Christian music and songs which were primarily designed for worship. Pete Ward quotes an Anglican report on the charismatic movement as observing, 'A creative talent has been unleashed and all and sundry now write their praises and their prayers to be sung as new songs' (Ward, 1996:120). Songs appeared courtesy of anyone who could 'strum a guitar or bash a drumset' (Page, 2004:17). This 'folk art', the work of the people, reflected the charismatic emphasis upon community and the notion that all could participate in the life and ministry of the church (Ward, 2005:185). Published in 1974, *Sound of Living Waters* contained many, early examples of the new songs.

Sound of Living Waters

Sound of Living Waters was the editorial work of Jeanne Harper and the American, Betty Pulkingham and part of their task was to gather up some of the fruits of charismatic creativity in the late 1960s and early 1970s. Their inclusion in *Sound of Living Waters* is indicated by songs which have no known author. Of the one hundred and thirty three songs in *Sound of Living Waters*, twenty eight were of this character. These and other new songs set out a musical path upon which charismatic Christianity was to journey over the following years. The emphasis upon worship and praise for example, which became characteristic of charismatic song, is reflected here. Ward's analysis reveals:

> *Sound of Living Waters* is primarily concerned with worship rather than teaching. This is reflected in the way songs are gathered into a number of sections. These include titles such as: 'Hallelujah! ......songs of praise and thanksgiving', 'Kneel and Adore .....songs of hope and vision.'
>
> (Ward, 2005:129)

That this sensibility is prominent can be seen from the fact that the editors described the entire collection of songs as a 'manual of praise' (Harper and Pulkingham, 1974: Foreword).

Sound of Living Waters also set a course in terms of the kind of musical genre that would come to typify worship songs. Although the collection is wide ranging and includes traditional material, there is an emphasis upon a certain folk synthesis including pop and traditional elements. The song book includes simple guitar chords which would have been familiar to folk or pop guitarists, (Ward, 2005:127) whilst the inclusion of a 'Choirmaster's Guide' at the rear, suggests a more traditional emphasis upon choral singing. That those responsible for *Sound of Living Waters* imagined this kind of folk fusion to be the default musical style of the collection is perhaps best seen by their relationship with the Fisherfolk. This worship group came from the same Houston church as Betty Pulkingham and in the early 1970s they toured the United Kingdom with her (Ward, 1996:122). Something of their impact can be seen by the fact that people could refer to songs, later to be published in *Sound of Living Waters*, as 'Fisherfolk type choruses' (Ward, 1996:120). The Fisherfolk sound, incorporating trained voices, gentle folk, with occasional pop rhythms, reflected very accurately the music style of *Sound of Living Waters*.

The lyrical structure of many of the new songs in *Sound of Living Waters* was also to be significant for the future. One of their key characteristics was simplicity. Ward for example, refers to a song entitled 'Alleluia' which is simply the title repeated eight times (Ward, 1996:126). Although an extreme example, in the first two sections of the book, in which the focus is especially on praise and worship, there are four others with a main verse comprised of no more than twenty five words (Harper, Pulkingham, 1974:song numbers 1, 10, 14, 26). Equally instructive, are the songs in which a basic pattern is repeated in a slightly different way. For example, the first verse of 'Oh! How good is the Lord' contains the lyrics:

> Oh! Oh! Oh! how good is the Lord
> Oh! Oh! Oh! how good is the Lord
> Oh! Oh! Oh! how good is the Lord
> I never will forget what he has done for me.
> (Anon. Arr. Harper and Pulkingham, 1974:22)

The other verses retain 'how good is the Lord' and the last line, but replace 'Oh Oh Oh' with such phrases as 'He gives me salvation' and 'He gives me his Spirit'. Of the thirty three songs in the praise and worship sections there are ten which reflect this style (Harper, Pulkingham, 1974:song numbers 4, 6, 13, 14, 19, 20, 21, 25, 26, 27). Ward attempts to explain the origin of the simple lyric by pointing to the desire for freedom within charismatic worship: 'The simplification of song lyrics enabled people to do without songbooks, so arms could be raised in praise or eyes closed in prayer' (Ward, 1996:127). These practical concerns may well have been involved to some extent. But the fact that lyrics remained fairly simple, when modern technology, through projectors of various sorts, removed the need for songs books, suggests that there is more to this than Ward suggests. A more likely scenario is suggested by Nick Page, who argues that worships songs imitated the simple lyrics of pop (Page, 2004:36-41). This is supported by Graham Kendrick who argued that the 'light' content was due to dominance of the 'three and a half minute pop song' (Kendrick, 2003:88).

Along with simple structures, *Sound of Living Waters* also presented a number of scripture songs, in which the exact words of the bible, or close paraphrases, make up all or a substantial part of a piece. One such example is 'We see the Lord', which is based on Isaiah 6:1:

> We see Jesus.
> We see the Lord,
> We see Jesus.
> We see the Lord,
> And he is high, he is high, high and lifted up,
> And his train fills the temple.
> He is high, he is high, high and lifted up,
> And his train fills the temple.
> The Angels cry 'Holy',
> The Angels cry 'Holy',
> The Angels cry 'Holy',
> The Angels cry 'Holy',
> The Angels cry 'Holy is the Lord'
> The Angels cry 'Holy is the Lord.'
> (Anon. Arr. Betty Pulkingham, 1974:48-49)

While these kind of songs indicated the importance of scripture to charismatics, by using words that were not in common use or would not be well understood, like 'holy' and 'train' in the above for example, they also infused a traditional element into the songs. This non-modern component is compounded in some cases, by the use of wording from the King James Version of the bible; song number eighty eight for example, is called 'Ho! everyone that thirsteth' (Harper, Pulkingham, 1974:152-153). This use of biblical language and old English was extraordinary given the concern for contemporary expressions of faith which marked the period. The growth in modern translations of the bible, signalled by J. B. Philips work on the New Testament in the late 1950s, reflected this theme, so too did the new hymn writing which can be found in the various hymn supplements of the late 1960s onwards. As the church music critic, Alan Luff, acknowledged, the Anglican and Methodist supplements 'concentrate on finding new words' even if new tunes were not available (Luff, *New Christian*, 13 November 1969:12). Some of the new worship songs indicated a move against this trend.

Sound of the Future

Although *Sound of Living Waters* established a synthesis that was to be influential for the future development of charismatic song, it was not an entirely static tradition. The choral element faded, as pop sounds took a more prominent role. This was encouraged by the influence of the *Praise* series of LPs which began in 1974. They owed much to Tommy Coomes, who had been a founder member of Love Song, an influential Jesus Movement pop group in the United States. Echoing artists like the Beach Boys and the Mama and the Papas, Love Song's sweet harmonies helped contribute to the 'mellow glow' of their music (Alfonso, 2002:192-193). As a record producer, Coomes helped export something of that warm pop sound to the *Praise* series. It helped lay the foundation for the increasing popularity of worship songs during the 1980s. The song writer, Chris Bowater, one of the leading figures in charismatic praise during this decade, noticed the increasing emulation of a 'pop culture that was lyrical, melodic and passionate' (Bowater, correspondence

11 April 2005). His reference to the 'lyrical' nature of praise and worship during this period is probably over stated. Yet, it cannot be doubted that in some cases it did escape the simplicities of the pop lyric. Most notable, was the work of Graham Kendrick, some of whose songs reflected a word seriousness which told of his roots as a folk singer. Nevertheless, the pop style lyric and the traditional element represented by the scripture song was still a strong feature in the tradition, as can be seen from any song collection of the period, such as *Songs of Fellowship* (Kingsway Publications, 2003) and the criticisms of the author Nick Page. Despite being a supporter of the genre, the latter argued for a more thoughtful, poetic lyricism (Page, 2004). Nor, did the essential musical focus change. In his *Encyclopedia of Contemporary Christian Music*, Mark Allan Powell concludes that the essential folk style of charismatic praise persisted, with little alteration for the next two decades (Powell, 2002:672).

The song of praise and worship represents the most enduring appropriation of 1960s youth music. One key reason for its success may have been its inclusive style. Although sourced from the folk boom of the 1960s, its gentle fusion of pop and traditional elements was never at the cutting edge of youth music and had a wide appeal. In his account of the worship of the Restoration churches, James Steven draws attention to its 'middle-of-the-road' musical style and how this was seen as a positive feature by many within the movement. This was because of its ability to connect with a wide range of people (Steven, 2003:19). While not one of the traditional Protestant denominations, Restoration's links with the wider charismatic movement suggests that this was a common validation of praise and worship musical style. Indeed, regard for an inclusive church music, points once more to *Sound of Living Waters*. It is a theme that is reflected in the editors catholic choice of song:

> The ocean is deep and wide; so also is the musical scope of this book. This volume is not limited by period or style, confined to

'youth songs' or content with 'old favourites'. Simply to turn a page may transport you from the measured dignity of Handel to the swinging rock beat of *Godspell*. We believe that both have their place in a mid-twentieth century manual of praise.

(Pulkingham and Harper, 1978:Foreward)

The concern for inclusivity, was, like other features we have noted in *Sound of Living Waters,* to prove programmatic for the character of the praise and worship song. The attractiveness of a folk fusion of pop and traditional elements lay in its ability to unite a diverse range of people. Significantly different from the traditional worship of organ and choir, its echo of youth style made it attractive for some young people, while the absence of an aggressive rock style element meant it could appeal to older generations.

This chapter has shown the wide ranging way in which the church responded to the folk boom of the second half of the 1960s. Folk music was extremely popular and was appropriated by all sides of the church. But the significance of folk is best seen in the uses to which it was put. It was used to reflect concerns about the world, to communicate the message about Jesus Christ and in public worship. At various points, I have also noted reasons why folk was seen as such an attractive proposition. For Christians concerned about the state of the world it had associations with protest. For those concerned with outreach it had connotations of relevance. For evangelical performers its strength lay in its word seriousness. Its relevance for worship was based around its ability to strengthen faith and unsettle it. For charismatics developing a new sound for worship, the appeal lay in its inclusivity.

4

Solid Rock

In previous chapters, I have demonstrated how Christian pop and to a much greater extent Christian folk fusions, found their way into the worshipping life of congregations during the 1960s and beyond. There was to be no such accommodation with rock music. This scenario might be seen as evidence confirming the views of social historians, such as Linda Martin, Kerry Segrave, Martin Cloonan and John Street, that ecclesial authorities and congregations were singularly opposed to such music. Certainly, those who were opposed to any kind of electric youth music in church would not have welcomed rock style. It was equally the case, that those who were motivated to create inclusive music, which moved charismatic song in the direction of a folk pop fusion, would not have found it an attractive option. Loud guitar or keyboard solos would not have been regarded as having a unifying function. Moreover, these characteristics of rock music were seen as problematic for those who valued the singing of hymns and songs as a key expression of congregational participation. Its stress on solos and performance deemed it unfit for worshipful purposes (Wren, 2000:166). Indeed, it was not until the 1990s that rock style sensibilities began to be reflected in worship through the reinvigoration of the worship song (Powell, 2002:251, 672).

Despite its long absence from church worship, this chapter will show that Christian reactions to early rock music were not entirely negative. From the late 1960s, evangelical Christians appropriated rock music and took it to concert halls, pubs and clubs. The increasing popularity of this type of music among evangelical youth will be observed through three important artists. In considering the beginnings of Christian rock music special attention will be given to the band, Out of Darkness. In terms of its increasing profile, our attention will focus on the American, Larry Norman. The group After the Fire will also concern us, as they represent the high point of this genre during the 1970s. Special attention will also be given to these artists motives for performing in secular venues. The absence of rock music in Christian worship might indicate that this was prompted by church hostility and that excluded from congregational worship, musicians were left with no other option but to take their music to the world. Such a scenario whilst not directly supporting the views of Martin, Segrave, Cloonan and Street would suggest that a very deep hostility existed between the church and its rock musicians. My purpose is not to deny that suspicion and misunderstanding occurred, or that unwelcoming churches contributed to the move to secular venues, it is to show that it was not the primary factor which motivated young evangelicals to take their music into the world.

Out of Darkness

By the end of 1960s, there were a number of Christian bands who were reflecting the soloing guitar style of Cream and Jimmy Hendrix. If the earlier Christian rhythm and blues bands stood on the edge of rock style, these fully entered that territory. They were not great in number. Tim Anderson, who played in a number of Christian groups during the 1960s remembers only a handful, the most important, of which he was a member, was Out of Darkness (Anderson, correspondence, 02 April 2007). Out of Darkness was a 'Gospel Blues Super Group', with musicians chosen by audition (Plankton Records, 2005). Their manager, Ian Wilkie, created the group out of some of the best musical talent available from the Christian music scene. Anderson, the drummer, came from the rhythm and blues band Insight, the vocalist and guitarist Tony Goodman, came from the Pilgrims. The two other members were Denver Grant on bass and Wray Powell, who could play in a Hendrix blues guitar style. Both were British Jamaicans and had previously been part of the black gospel group the Soul Seekers. As Anderson, who went on to lecture in popular music at Southwark College, commented, they were not a typical gospel ensemble:

> There were very few black gospel groups in the UK in the 1960s and they were mainly vocal harmony groups such as the Sacred Sisters, the Golden Chords and the Singing Stewarts. The Soul Seekers were probably one of the first to feature drums and guitars and certainly the first to look like a black beat group.
>
> (Anderson, correspondence, 02 April 2007)

If the multicultural mix of Out of Darkness was a novel and for some, a disturbing element in the late 1960s and early 1970s, (*Cross Rhythms*, Issue 23, October/November 1994, Long, 2004), the result of their musical enterprise was also something new, a genuine rock album produced by a Christian band.

Gospel Blues

In 1969, Out of Darkness was signed by the MGO record label Key and the following year saw the release of their eponymous debut album. The adoption of a hard edged, modern rock style clearly indicated that they were pioneers within the world of Christian music. Over thirty years later, the flavour of the album and the reverence with which some Christian commentators still regard it, can be sensed by the words of Ken Scott, an American Jesus music expert:

> This is the one folks! Heavy duty progressive hard rock scorcher with tons of loud blistering guitar work which gets incredibly spastic at times as on 'Closin' In On Me'. Must have been the

gutsiest thing ever released on a Christian label at the time. Nods to 70s sounds of Hendrix, Cream, punchy Stones rhythm guitar, playing the gamut of styles, too: 'Lemonade and Peanuts' is loud blues/beat with a wailing harmonica, psychedelic folk is explored on 'Homeland' and 'Hustle Bustle' features some nifty jazz-influenced guitar.

(Scott, 2003:101)

Despite the affinities with popular rock sounds, Out of Darkness did not see their music as derivative of any secular band or performer. They were however, part of a growing enthusiasm for a sound which was inspired by black American blues music. Included in this genre was the style of gospel blues. Noticing that secular British bands such as Alexis Corner, Long John Baldry and even the Rolling Stones and Led Zeppelin included gospel blues numbers in their sets, Out of Darkness reasoned that it was 'quite natural for Christian musicians to play their own version of gospel blues' (Anderson, correspondence, 02 April 2007). Among their key influences were Ray Charles and Sister Rosetta Tharpe, the latter, although not so well known as Charles, was particularly important.

Sister Rosetta Tharpe was born in Cotton Plant, Arkansas on 21 March, 1921. Although little is known of her early life, in later years she told of appearing with her mother, holiness evangelist, Katie Bell Nubin and performing before thousands in her youth (Darden, 2004:197). She developed a unique style which reflected her gospel roots but which also drew heavily upon the blues. This was perhaps most evident through her electric guitar playing. At a time when few women played the instrument, Tharpe's playing was skilful and aggressive (Darden, 2004:199). Signed by the Decca label in 1938, she quickly became a huge success. Darden's glowing tribute, offers an idea of the impact she made:

She was the Madonna of her day – fearlessly challenging roles and costumes and social mores. She was the Dolly Parton of her day –

irrepressible, unfazed by criticism, a sexy girl from the country. She was the Queen Latifah of her day – larger than life, lavishly talented, able to move between seemingly irreconcilable worlds with consummate ease.

(Darden, 2004:197)

The reference to 'irreconcilable worlds' points to the difficulty of trying to keep her core church audience happy, while at the same time taking her music out into the world. Devout listeners accused her of 'selling out' by recording secular songs and were unhappy with her performing in what were regarded as 'venues of iniquity' (Livin Blues, 2007). This came to a head in the early 1950s when she recorded some blues songs. Although Tharpe maintained her evangelical message was unaltered; she alienated her church constituency. Consequently, she turned to Europe and was the first major gospel singer to tour the continent and continued to be successful there throughout the 1960s (Livin Blues, 2007). In 1970, three members of Out of Darkness went to see her in concert, at what turned out to be her last in the United Kingdom. Although they knew of her music, Tim Anderson was surprised by her 'virtuoso guitar playing' and that she used feedback 'just like Hendrix' (Anderson, correspondence, 30 April 2007). For him and the others, it 'confirmed that they were on the right track' (Anderson, correspondence, 30 April 2007). Out of Darkness determined to carry on the tradition of gospel blues.

For those unaware of where Out of Darkness located their inspiration, it was natural to think that they were appropriating the style of popular secular rock bands. Indeed, given the impact of Cream, the Rolling Stones and Jimmy Hendrix for example, one can not discount their influence on Out of Darkness. It must also be said, that in attempting to contemporise gospel blues they were moving in the same broad musical direction as secular bands who attempted the same kind of thing in their repertoire. The sound of Out of Darkness was then, very much in keeping with a rock sound of the late 1960s and early

1970s. However, the tradition did have some distinctive implications for how they worked as a band and for the kind of message they communicated.

Method and Message

One recurring feature of those who performed gospel blues was a desire to take the music out of the church and into the world. Sister Rosetta Tharpe's willingness to release secular songs in a gospel blues style and to take her music to what were regarded as inappropriate venues is a perfect example of this. It was a feature which could be expressed in a more radical direction. For example, Ray Charles, another of Out of Darkness influences, used the churchy piano and the worshipful moans of gospel, but abandoned the spiritual focus completely (Turner, 1988:50). He harnessed gospel's emotional power to earthbound stories of what he would later call 'love heartaches, money heartaches, pleasure of the flesh and pleasures of the soul' (cited in Turner, 1988:50). Words which spoke of devotion to the Lord were exchanged for lyrics which spoke of love for a woman. Charles' transfer of gospel sounds from the church to the world was achieved in an entirely secular direction. He did not perform religious songs (Turner, 1988:51). Tharpe however, continued to sing gospel lyrics and to take their message into the world. In 1941 for example, she explained that her mission was to 'save souls' and that she sang in night clubs because 'there are more souls that need saving in the niteries than there are in the church' (cited in Wald, 2007:53). In this aspect, it was her example, rather than that of Charles, that was important for Out of Darkness. The band performed their Christian songs before largely secular audiences. Although they did play at Christian concerts and coffee bars, their main emphasis was upon sharing their music and message with those who did not share their faith (Goodman, correspondence, 13 August 2005). Night clubs, dance halls and concert arenas were preferred to church based events. Out of Darkness performed at venues which were focal points for the white expression of blues music, these included the prestigious Flamingo, Marquee and Ricky-Tick clubs in London (Goodman, correspondence, 13 August 2005, *Cross Rhythms*, Issue 23, October/November 1994, Long, 2004). By playing their music before largely secular audiences Out of Darkness continued in the tradition of gospel blues. It was understood to have evangelistic potential, as vocalist Tony Goodman reported, it was thought to be 'a great way to present the gospel to those never going near a church' (Tony Goodman, correspondence, 13 August 2005). As gospel blues influenced the type of venues in which Out of Darkness performed it also informed the content of their lyrics.

Out of Darkness songs frequently reflected blues themes of realism and of a world characterised by misery and tears. Their LP record included songs about a poor neglected six year old ('Lemonade and peanuts'), hypocrisy ('Who is to blame') and various sorts of people whose desperate need is ignored ('There you see a stranger'). Even more, there are songs which feature powerful testimonies of individuals struggling with darkness. 'Closing in on me' for example, has the following refrain:

> I can feel the world outside closing in on me
> I can feel the world Oh Lord, it's trying to get to me
> I can tell by the things I'm thinking
> The thoughts running through my mind
> Oh I can feel the world Oh Lord closing in on me
> Yeh, yeh, yeh.
>
> (Powell, 1970:track 7)

These lyrics allow Out of Darkness to enter fully into the blues. But they are also framed in such a way as to convey the Christian message. Ultimately, the songs reveal that the answer to the blues and indeed darkness is to be found in Christ. Some of the words from the song 'On Solid Rock' for example, reflect this theme:

> Although my life is but a breath,
> Just a passing shadow,
> God's deep concern reached out to me,
> Like the sunshine through my window
>
> Oh who am I that God should hear my cry?
> And stoop down to dry my tears?
> Yet in my heart I feel a deep warm glow
> Dispelling all those doubts and fears.
> (Powell and Goodman, 1970:track 3)

The favoured format to describe the remedy for the blues was the testimony song. Of the thirteen songs on the album (one is a short instrumental piece), eight tell a story of release and redemption from the point of view of the first person singular. Along with Malcolm and Alwyn and other evangelical artists, but preceding them, Out of Darkness developed a style which contemporised the traditional evangelical emphasis on individual transformation. As with the case of Malcolm and Alwyn, it may well reflect a concern with personal change that was abroad in society at the time. Certainly, Out of Darkness contrasted the benefits of faith with alternative means of personal transformation. In the song 'On Solid Rock', the singer claims that Christian faith means there is now 'no need to escape to the dreamer's mystic land' (Powell, Goodman, 1970:track 3). The precise meaning of the phrase is unclear; it could refer to those who pursued alternative spiritualities, drugs or even hedonism as a means of self fulfillment. The phrase is general enough to cover all these activities and perhaps this was its purpose. If this was the situation, it suggested that those life style choices commonly associated with personal liberation were nothing more than a form of escapism, embraced so as to avoid harsh worldly realities. By way of contrast, the song suggested that only the gospel actually enabled one to face grim reality and to cope with it. As the band's name suggested there was a way out of darkness, as their lyrics reveal, it came through the message about Jesus Christ.

Out of Darkness changed their line up in the early 1970s as Tony Goodman left. With the growing influence of lead guitarist Wray Powell, they created a sound even more reminiscent of Jimmy Hendrix. But unable to find a record deal with a major company they disbanded in 1974 (*Cross Rhythms*, Issue 23, October/November 1994, Long, 2004). By that time the evangelical sub-culture had come under the influence of Larry Norman, who probably did more than any other person to popularise rock style within the constituency.

Larry Norman

Larry Norman is commonly regarded as the singular most important figure in the development of Christian contemporary music. Often described as the 'the father of Christian rock music', his album, *Upon this Rock*, is frequently cited as the first Christian rock album (see for example, Powell 2002:633-634, Webb, 2006:35-36). Although I have already questioned the first of these accolades by focusing on Out of Darkness and will shortly dispute the second, there is little doubt that he was a highly influential performer. His drawing on the blues, with strong echoes of Bob Dylan and Mick Jagger, made him a revered figure in parts of evangelical youth culture.

Upon this Rock

Norman was born in Corpus Christi, Texas, in 1947, but grew up in a mainly black area of San Francisco. He quickly showed unusual musical talent and began creating his own songs from the age of five. (Norman, 2002:sleeve notes). He was particularly affected by blues, black gospel sounds and Elvis. (Norman, 2002:sleeve notes, Alfonso, 2002:209). Born into a devout, conservative Christian family, he did not have a 'conversion experience' like many of those in the Jesus Movement who performed youth music. Indeed, the trajectory of Norman's life was not from hippie culture to the church, but the other way around (Powell, 2002:633). Mark Allen Powell describes Norman's appropriation of 1960s American youth culture:

> Norman came as a young Christian to embrace parts of the counter-cultural youth movement, while clearly rejecting other aspects of it. He never did drugs and he was not noted for protesting the Vietnam war or for supporting civil rights. He did however, grow his hair down to his waist and learn to play 'protest songs' of Dylanesque stature. He spoke in the idiom of the day (minus obscenities) and he espoused enough anti-institutionalism and showed sufficient disrespect for (selected) authorities to earn him a place in the hearts of America's hippie youth. Most of all he embraced rock and roll, which was completely absent from the liturgies of virtually all churches.
>
> (Powell, 2002:633)

At the age of eighteen Norman created a band called People, which he then left after a dispute with his record company. He then wrote and staged two musicals before releasing the album *Upon this Rock*.

Upon this Rock was released in 1969 and in many ways reflected the psychedelic music of the late 1960s, typical of the Beatles on *Sgt. Pepper's Lonely Heart Club Band*. Unconventional arrangements of songs such as a loud, discordant piano on 'The last Supper' and the juxtaposition of shrieking orchestral sings with sweet female voices in 'Moses in the Wilderness' point in this direction. A debt to the blues is also evident. Norman's lyrics and delivery sometimes evoke a sense of menace that all is not well with the world. In 'I don't believe in miracles' for example, Norman writes of someone struggling with belief:

> I don't believe in miracles.
> I know what's real I don't pretend
> I don't believe in miracles
> Or stories with a happy end
> Life is no ones friend ………
>
> I don't believe in miracles
> I've been around I've seen enough
> The only way to get along you must be strong
> You must be tough, life is one big bluff.
>
> (Norman, 1969:track 2)

Although Norman's lyric goes on to present an answer to this dark perspective, the sense of overwhelming futility with which he delivers the words is convincing. There are elements then, which reflect a rock sensibility. In general terms however, *Upon the Rock* is rather too mellow to fall within this category. It contains bright, sing-a-long pop numbers like 'Sweet, Sweet Song of Salvation' and 'Nothing Really Changes'. The production includes orchestral arrangements and the most frequently heard instrument is the acoustic guitar. Most significantly, it contains not a solitary electric guitar solo. In the sleeve notes for the reissue of *Upon this Rock* in 2002, Norman acknowledges the relative sweetness of the production (he had actually wanted to make a much edgier piece of music) and an interesting retrospective:

> Looking back 33 years, I must say that I'm rather happy that the album sounded so benign instead of embodying the ferocious rock statement I wanted to make. The album 'travelled well' into other cultures and slipped behind walls of defence which would have kept out my version; to protect their innocent children from the corruption of rock.
>
> (Norman, 2002:sleeve notes)

Upon this Rock may not have been the first fully fledged rock album but his subsequent albums moved more in a rock direction. In 1972, the release of *Only Visiting this Planet* for example, still gave a high profile to folk blues but also included guitar led rock numbers.

Rock Star

Norman's popularity in the United Kingdom was enhanced by a period in the early 1970s when he lived in London and performed across the country. His first tour in the spring of 1972 saw him give thirty eight concerts in thirty five days (Official Larry Norman UK Website, 2004). It began in Lancaster University and this was the type of secular venue that was to characterise his live performances. In 1975 for example, his twelve date British tour included only two ecclesiastical settings (Bristol Cathedral and Westminster Central Hall), while he also appeared on a number of occasions at the Royal Albert Hall in London during the early 1970s (Official Larry Norman UK Website, 2004). Performing in churches was not a significant feature of Norman's work, like Out of Darkness he preferred to take his music out into the world. I will argue that this is best understood as a consequence of his taking the role of the archetypal rock star. Such persons, of course, are not generally known for performing in church. But exploration of this theme begins by noticing the unconventional nature, at least as far as evangelicals were concerned, of Norman's musical message.

By the late 1960s, evangelicals had become familiar with the idea of using youth music as a tool of outreach; Larry Norman's music did not fit this pattern. It was not that he did not perform material which challenged people to believe, but that there were so many other types of song. An album like *Only Visiting this Planet,* released in 1972 and produced by George Martin, illustrated how diverse was his range. 'Why Don't You Look into Jesus' is the one song which directly addresses the unbeliever to change. Norman presents himself as an evangelist inviting his listeners to find that Jesus is the 'answer'. But along with the role of evangelist Norman takes other roles, as a preacher, encouraging the church to embrace rock 'n' roll in 'Why Should the Devil have all the Good Music', more darkly, 'I Wish We'd All Been Ready', casts him as apocalyptic prophet warning of the imminent return of Jesus Christ. In the song 'The Great American Novel', Norman takes the part of a Dylan style protest singer complaining about a wide range of things including racism, the cost of the space programme and American foreign policy. 'Readers Digest', contains acidic musings on popular culture, in particular the early 1970s music scene and refers among other things, to John Lennon's comment about the Beatles being more popular than Jesus and rumours that Paul McCartney was dead:

> Alice is a drag queen
> Bowie's somewhere in between
> Other bands are looking mean
> Me I'm trying to stay clean
> I don't dig the radio
> I hate what the charts pick
> Rock and roll may not be dead
> But it's getting sick
> All over the world
> Disc jockeys sound the same
> And every town I play
> Is like the one from where I came
> The Rolling Stones are millionaires
> Flower children pallbearers
> Beatles said all 'all you need is love'
> And then they broke up
> Jimi took an overdose Janis followed so close
> The whole music scene
> And all the bands are pretty comatose

This time last year
People didn't wanna hear
They looked at Jesus from afar
Now they call him 'superstar'
Dear John who's more popular now
I've been listening to some of Paul's new records
Sometimes I think he really is dead.

(Norman, 1972:track 10)

To this role of social observer can be added that of blues singer, 'I've Got to Learn to Live Without You' and 'Pardon Me' talk about the pain of broken relationships without any kind of reference to God or Jesus. For those who were interested in Christian youth music, Norman's diverse repertoire raised questions about his purpose. When Norman was interviewed by Steve Goddard and Roger Green for *Buzz* magazine in 1981, the first questions were all concerned with how the artist understood his work (Goddard, Green, *Buzz*, May 1981, Official Larry Norman UK Website, 2004).

If the readers of Goddard and Green had been hoping to discover the musical model on which Norman based his work they would probably have been disappointed, as his comments were far from straight forward. Asked about the 'aim' of his ministry, Norman suggested that his music was not a ministry, 'just a bunch of notes' (Goddard, Green, *Buzz*, May 1981, Official Larry Norman UK Website, 2004). Later in the interview, when discussing the consequences of his recent divorce, however, he could talk of 'my ministry'. Norman admitted that he was trying to say 'A lot of things' through his songs, including speaking of Christ to an unbelieving culture, yet, he can later say that he never achieved evangelism through his music; 'Music is art, not propaganda' he declared (Goddard, Green, *Buzz*, May 1981, Official Larry Norman UK Website, 2004). The interviewees were not impressed by the whole experience, they wrote in an explanatory piece:

At times it was difficult to remember who was actually doing the interview. Some questions were thrown back at us in a defensive manner and when we received a reply it was at the third time of asking.

(Goddard, Green, *Buzz*, May 1981, Official Larry Norman UK Website, 2004)

While the interview might have done little to clarify the rationale of Norman's work in an explicit sense, its character is revealing, bearing the hallmarks of the difficult to interview rock musician. The Beatles and Bob Dylan had been involved in such discourses, it appeared that Norman was continuing in this tradition (for an example of the Beatles' sarcasm and wit, see Trynka, 2004:215-217, for Dylan's awkwardness, see *Disc Weekly*, 22 May 1965:6, *NME Originals*, Vol.2, Issue 5:20-21). In his *Encyclopedia of Contemporary Christian Music*, Mark Allan Powell suggests that Norman exhibited:

The qualities of a stereotypical 'rock artist' personality – mysterious, dismissive, manipulative – but, above all, possessed with an undisputed genius that would consistently set him beyond the comprehension or reach of those who would offer (sometimes legitimate) criticisms of his life and work.

(Powell, 2002:633)

His stage presence underlined the rock star image. His long blonde hair, unsmiling face, black shirt and jeans did not 'conform to the image of the happy guitar strumming singer for Jesus' (Alfonso, 2002:210). Instead, it spoke of a style which 'could have come straight out of the biography of a world famous rock star' (Goddard, Green, *Buzz*, May 1981, Official Larry Norman UK Website, 2004).

Norman himself appears to have been rather unhappy with some of the consequences of his Christian rock star role. In the 1981 interview he argued that he was not an exceptional person, just an 'ordinary guy', didn't spend time worrying about 'image', didn't sign autographs and was dismissive of those who were preoccupied with keeping their Christian record collection up to date. He even went so far as to hope that such people would be so inspired to care for the poor that they would have no time to listen to Christian music and have no money to spend on it (Goddard, Green, *Buzz*, May 1981, Official Larry Norman UK Website, 2004). To what extent these things were genuinely part of Norman's perspective is a matter of conjecture, Goddard and Green hint that it might have been part of a strategy to present himself as an 'anti-hero'. Whatever, it highlighted the propensity for controversy which marked Norman's career and which reflected the role of the outspoken Christian rock star.

Rock Influence

Larry Norman may not have been the founding father of Christian rock, nor the first to have produced a Christian rock album, but he was the first Christian to appear who looked and behaved like a rock star and was an important figure in the development of Christian youth music. As a key performer and the supposed originator of Christian rock he has been the subject of much hyperbole. For example, Goddard and Green begin their 1981 interview with Norman by saying:

> There is little doubt that every Christian music punter and performer from After the Fire to the local youth fellowship band, owe it to Larry for nailing the myth that it wasn't righteous to rock 'n' roll.
>
> (Goddard, Green, *Buzz*, May 1981, Official Larry Norman UK Website, 2004)

Given what other British groups had been doing before Norman arrived in the United Kingdom such claims appear rather overstated. Certainly, there were few who came along attempting to imitate his sound. This was probably because

Norman's own music was derivative of Dylan and Jagger and these primary references were always more likely to be mentioned than Norman's work. It is also true, that with the passing of time his sound began to appear somewhat dated. Indeed, the increasing appeal of middle of the road, praise and worship music within Evangelicalism provides another indicator that Norman's impact was far from overwhelming. Nevertheless, there is ample evidence of his impact on those who listened and watched. Those who acknowledge his influence include general artists as diverse as U2, John Mellencamp and Frank Black (the leader of the alternative rock group the Pixies). Black was raised on Norman's music and even admits to having once won a Larry Norman Look-Alike Contest (Powell, 2002:633, 640). Over three hundred different artists have covered Norman's songs. His impact on Christian musicians in Great Britain during the 1970s is perhaps best seen through his involvement with Malcolm and Alwyn and Cliff Richard.

Malcolm and Alwyn have already been featured in this study as purveyors of modern evangelical folk style. This accurately describes much of their first album, and their second, *Wildwall*, also reflected this style to some extent. But there is also a much rockier, edgier feel to this album which includes chiming electric guitar riffs and unconventional arrangements using studio technology. It is a good deal more sophisticated than their debut LP and Powell attributes this change to Norman (Powell, 2002:557). Although Norman did not produce the record, there is a strong likelihood that it reflected his influence. The two parties had toured together during Norman's sojourn in England during the early 1970s and Norman was clearly an admirer of the duo, even writing a song about them entitled 'Dear Malcolm, Dear Alwyn'. Given Norman's reputation at the time, it would be surprising if this relationship did not bear some fruit in the way Malcolm and Alwyn constructed their music. It may also be possible that the American's influence extended beyond that of music. Malcolm and Alwyn seldom addressed social or political issues, on *Wildwall* there is only one song which can be said to fall into this category. 'Spaceman' is concerned with what is considered to be the futility of the space programme. The song considers the joy of riding on the moon while people back on earth are fighting and 'wondering if they'll get another meal' (Wild/Wall, 1974:track 3). At another point they argue: 'No use being friendly with Martians, If you can't be friendly with your brother, And making the acquaintance of little green men, While black and white are fighting each other'. It is perhaps significant, that on the one occasion that the duo should address wider matters they should focus on the subject of the space programme. It was one of Norman's favourite topics during the time that he was resident in the United Kingdom and sharing platforms with Malcolm and Alwyn. The album, *Only Visiting this Planet,* produced during this period, had a number of references to the issue. Of course, concerns about the validity of the space programme, was not unusual among those who had affinities with youth counter-culture and it is entirely possible that Malcolm and Alwyn were merely reflecting this concern. On the other hand, it seems most likely that Norman may have been the source of inspiration for the lyrical content of this song as well as being a more general musical influence.

Cliff Richard announced that he had become a Christian during Billy Graham's mission to London in 1966. He subsequently seriously considered giving up his career in music (Turner, 2005:235ff). The evangelical Christianity he embraced, though changing, was still unsure about the merits of a Christian earning a living via the entertainment industry. Although Richard decided to stay with his music, there could be no disguising of the fact that it was in need of rejuvenation. Like many other artists, Richard's popularity had been affected by the success of the new music of the 1960s. Turner refers to a *Melody Maker* article on shifting musical tastes where a young 'beat fan' is quoted as commenting:

I grew out of my Cliff Richard days a couple of years ago. When I look back I think how soppy I must have been. Groups like the Beatles and the Stones have really got something and I can't see myself getting tired of them. Not until I'm old anyway.

(Turner, 2005:219)

From 1964, the volume of single sales steadily declined and following his public declaration of faith, the only huge hit Richard managed to achieve was with the British Eurovision entry 'Congratulations' in 1968. This identified Richard with a jaunty middle of the road sound, far removed from his rock 'n' roll roots and contemporary rock music. The overall trend of declining sales and increased musical irrelevance continued into the early 1970s. It appeared that Richard was 'destined to become a Tommy Steele or Frankie Vaughan type of entertainer who could always sell out a show but who no longer belonged on the top table' (Turner, 2005:265). But Richard himself appears to have been freshly motivated to turn things around; with the help of producers Dave Mackay and Bruce Welsh his career had been re-ignited by 1976. The album *I'm Nearly Famous*, brought him excellent reviews, new credibility and hit singles. It was to set Richard on a path which would see him continue to produce hit singles until the end of the millennium. Among those like Mackay and Welsh, who helped bring about this transformation, must also be numbered Norman. At the time Richard was thinking about his musical direction he was listening to Norman's music. He went to see him in concert at the Albert Hall and they later met and discussed some of the musical dilemmas that Richard faced (Turner, 2005:262-263). Norman's music was clearly an important influence during this key period. It proved to him that a Christian could perform contemporary music with integrity. Something of Norman's influence can be seen on *Small Corners*, a gospel album released in 1977. His first such release, *Goodnews* (1967), was comprised of spirituals, hymns and gospel songs. *Small Corners* had a much more contemporary feel about it and a quarter of the songs were covers of Norman compositions. The set of songs was headed with Norman's apologia for Christian rock music 'Why should the Devil have all the good music'.

The influence of Norman on other musicians and artists has been a significant part of his legacy to contemporary Christian music. For others, his influence was of a more general nature. Norman's charismatic personality and the potency of his sound and lyrics made him a popular figure among evangelical youth. People were passionate about his music, mouthing the lyrics to his songs as he performed in concert (Goddard, Green, *Buzz*, May 1981, Official Larry Norman UK Website, 2004). Although it is possible to exaggerate his importance, more than any other artist, he proved to evangelical youngsters that rock music and the Christian faith were not incompatible.

After the Fire

During the early 1970s, the amount of evangelical youth music multiplied. Pilgrim Records, MGO's label Key and the British arm of the American record company, Word, all began operating in the late 1960s and ensured that there was a number of different outlets for the new music. The number of bands increased enormously as can be seen from *Buzz* magazine's circulation of concerts and events. The growth in popularity of Christian youth music during the 1970s is best illustrated by the Greenbelt festival. When this showcase for evangelical engagement with the arts began in 1974, barely two thousand people attended, five years later the figure approached twenty thousand (Henderson, 1984:5, 52). The increasing taste for rock music, encouraged by the example of Out of Darkness and Larry Norman, was illustrated by the presence of the band, After the Fire (ATF). They were regularly visitors to Greenbelt between 1974 and 1979 and were absent only in 1974 and 1978.

After the Fire was the brain child of Peter Banks, a virtuoso key board player. First established in 1971, it quickly folded, but in 1974, Banks and the original drummer Ian Adamson started to put together a new group. This time around the results were more successful. By 1976, they had become one of the most acclaimed groups within evangelical youth culture, coming second in a *Buzz* magazine poll as the most appreciated artist or group of the year. The following year, *Buzz* readers put them level with Larry Norman as the most appreciated live act (Carr, 1999:chapter 11). By the time they appeared at Greenbelt in 1979, they had been signed by the CBS record label, changed their original musical style and had a small hit with their first single (Carr, 1999:chapter 13). They represented the height of Evangelicalism's success in its engagement with youth music. In what follows, I will focus on their earlier musical incarnation, which reflected a very particular late 1960s style and describe the nature of their interaction with the world of secular music.

Signs of Change

After the Fire's first album, the independently produced *Sings of Change*, recorded in 1977, though not actually released until 1978, encapsulated the kind of music that After the Fire played during the middle part of the 1970s. It was a musical style which mimicked the progressive rock music of the era, begun in the late 1960s by the likes of King Crimson, The Nice and Genesis, which fused traditional classical music with rock sounds. According to Banks, another prominent band of the era, Emerson, Lake and Palmer, was the primary musical inspiration for the early After the Fire (Peter Banks, correspondence, 11 November 2005). Typical of the genre, the songs they played were invariably of long duration. *Signs of Change* contained only six songs and the final track, 'Pilgrim', was over eleven minutes long. After the Fire's compositions were also marked by instrumental sections, changes in tempo and direction. Of their distinctive features, one of the most interesting was an element of folk. At certain points, some songs had a jig like quality, indeed *Signs of Change* contained an unusual instrumental piece entitled 'Jigs' which could have been produced by a traditional folk band. But there were other songs which reflected this sound. Most noticeable in this respect, was the previously mentioned track 'Pilgrim', which began with a jig excursion (almost two minutes), before travelling off in a rather different musical direction. That folk music should feature in After the Fire's musical mix was not entirely surprising. Banks had previously been part of a Christian group called Narnia, who produced an album entitled *Aslan is not a Tame Lion* in 1974. The band was fronted by the established folk singer Pauline Filby, who wrote most of the bands material. Consequently, the album had strong folk over- tones. At the same time, there was a real attempt to create a progressive rock sound. The other key member of ATF, lead vocalist and co-writer with Banks, Andy Piercy, had even deeper connections with folk music. He had played in folk clubs, and with Ian Smale had been part of the Christian folk duo, Ishmael and Andy. It would certainly be wrong to over-emphasize the importance of folk music for After the Fire. They delivered a sound which was unmistakably part of the prog rock genre, but the previous folk connections of their song writers shone through at various points and helped establish a distinctive sound.

Like Out of Darkness and Larry Norman, After the Fire tended to avoid explicit Christian venues like churches and church halls. They took their music to a secular circuit of colleges and universities, theatres, pubs and music clubs (Friends of After the Fire, 1999a). But if Out of Darkness were motivated to go out into the world by the tradition of gospel blues and Norman by his taking of the role of rock artist, After the Fire did so for other reasons. They were concerned to inhabit the world of secular music and win friends and influence people by the entirety of their life as a band. Banks declared; 'After the Fire's mission was to be salt and light out there in the world. It was a complete determination to be where folk who may have little or no connection to church were' (Peter Banks, correspondence, 11

November 2005). Such a policy indicated an increasing ease with modern culture which was a characteristic of certain evangelicals during this period. In David Bebbington's account of Evangelicalism, he noted how the 'introverted attitudes' of the 1940s, characterised among other things, by a suspicion of the world and the arts, began to change dramatically during the 1960s (Bebbington, 1989:263). Those sections of Evangelicalism which responded positively to the music of youth culture reflected this new approach. With After the Fire, however, came a deeper, more thorough going integration with the modern world, which set them apart from what had gone before. For all their appropriation of modern sounds, Christian groups like the Crossbeats and Out of Darkness gave the impression that the world outside the Christian community was a fairly dark place. Their style of musical evangelism could be characterised by commando like raids on enemy territory. The band performed, presented a message and then withdrew to the safety of their evangelical base. After the Fire on the other hand, were determined to locate themselves more thoroughly within the world of secular music and bring a Christian presence into the industry. Speaking in 1982, the founder of Greenbelt and singer with the Christian blues band All Things New, James Holloway, reflected on this changing sensibility:

> At the time it was becoming, increasingly accepted that if Christians could enjoy good music they could play it as well, and be involved in the business. This was a shift from justifying involvement in rock or pop by piously calling it a ministry (church jargon word that can cover almost anything); to simply needing no other reason than enjoyment or entertainment.
>
> (Holloway, *Strait 3*, January 1982, Friends of After the Fire, 1999b)

After the Fire did not play simply for the fun of it, but their willingness to situate themselves within the secular musical world was evidence of new attitudes within Evangelicalism.

Sowing Seeds

The images of salt and light which Banks used to describe After the Fire's role in the world were drawn from the New Testament and were essentially connected to the idea of Christian distinctiveness (France, 1985:112). Being true to such a vision involved a variety of challenges for After the Fire. In an interview with Lindsey Tuffin for *Buzz* magazine in 1977, they explained that this included dealing graciously with promoters who wouldn't pay what was owed them, demonstrating that they did not need drugs or alcohol to perform well and showing that it was possible for Christians to play rock music to skeptical musical journalists (Tuffin, *Buzz*, December 1977, Friends of After the Fire, 1999b). With respect to this latter goal, the interview revealed a variable degree of success. After the Fire quoted a review of their work by Miles of the music newspaper *New Musical Express,* who associated rock music with 'rebellion, sexual liberation and 'attacks on patriarchy and authoritarianism'. He thought it inconceivable that Christians could communicate the gospel through the medium (cited in Tuffin, *Buzz*, December 1977, Friends of After the Fire, 1999b). As can be seen from the introduction to this study, similar views would still be current over ten years later through scholars like John Street. However, other music commentators were rather more responsive, Chas De Whalley of *Sounds* newspaper commented:

> You will find them quite strangely un-derivative and fresh. Much to my surprise I found After the Fire remarkably enjoyable. Even on stage the four Fires seem to be one of the friendliest and unaffected bands in a long while.
>
> (cited in Tuffin, *Buzz*, December, 1977, Friends of After the Fire, 1999b)

It was this kind of response that After the Fire looked for from music business people and audiences. While the role of salt and light did not involve them in direct evangelism they did hope that it might be the means of encouraging a positive reaction to their faith. Peter Banks saw it as 'seed sowing', which was about creating an initial response which might eventually lead to greater things (Peter Banks, correspondence, 11 November 2005). The same theme of seed sowing can also be applied to their lyrics.

Although long instrumental sections punctuated After the Fire's songs, their lyrical content was also strong, it reflected a Bob Dylan inspired word seriousness, which was typical of rock bands during this period. In many ways, After the Fire's lyrics are similar to the testimony songs of Out of Darkness and Malcolm and Alwyn and feature songs written in the first person singular. But where as these earlier artists embraced a wide variety of personal stories, After the Fire offered only one model, which told of someone struggling to find purpose and meaning and engaging with the possibility that faith might provide the answer. The personal crisis song is usually resolved in favour of an acceptance of Christ. On *Signs of Change*, only two songs, the instrumental 'Jigs' and 'Pilgrim', did not follow this format. On the 2004 reissue of the album, the bonus tracks "Samaritan Women' and 'Dreamaway' also follow the same formulae involving someone weighing up the merits of faith. The extended format of the prog rock genre allowed After the Fire to introduce other 'voices' into the personal drama that their songs described. The title track of *Signs of Change*, for example, begins with an account of someone looking for a change of direction:

> Ever since my life began it's always been a bore
> Nothing ever happened much to me
> Always needed something else, that certain something more
> Who can tell me what that thing may be?
>
> If only I could find a way of changing what I am
> Maybe that's what I need to know?

But would it go and complicate some vast eternal plan
To re-direct the way I want to go?
                    (Piercy and Banks, 1978:track 4)

At this point, a strong, almost chant like refrain is heard which suggests that change is impossible:

Life must be taken the way that you find it
The die has been cast and the scene is set
Don't try to change it, just plod on regardless
Swallowing hard, taking what you get

The books are all written, the stars they all show it
You can only accept it that when you are born
And the sign you were under
Your life will dictate – you can't change it's too late!
                    (Piercy and Banks, 1978:track 4)

But the voice which commends the power of fate does not triumph. The main narrative voice continues and concludes with a rather different resolution:

Oh, no, please God there's more than this
Life's more than chance, won't you tell me it's true
What they say, that you can change a man
Forgive me, I'll live for you

I need a new start, is it too much to ask?
God who made the earth and sea
Won't you create a new heart in me?

You lifted me up and you dusted me down
You set my feet back on sold ground
The stars can no longer cause me pain
You've changed my sign, I've been born again.
                    (Piercy and Banks, 1978:track 4)

Other After the Fire songs, including "Back to the Light' and 'Dreamaway', are structured in this way and is evidence of a concern with literary seriousness.

Although After the Fire's Christian lyrics were not intended to force their faith upon their listeners, they did hope that they might sow some gospel seeds in people lives. As lead vocalist, Andy Piercy explained in 1978: 'In a live situation, one of our aims has been to win friends so they will buy an album and hear what we're saying' (Carr, 1999:chapter 12). The perception that an album was a key communicative device meant that acquiring a record deal was of great importance. After several offers of contracts, the band decided to produce and market an album themselves. *Signs of Change* was a largely 'in house' production. It received fairly positive reviews from the secular press and tracks were played on Radio One and on London's Capital Radio, but as an evangelistic tool it is doubtful whether it matched Piercy's ambition. The level of sales, reportedly two thousand copies in the first month, was poor by secular standards. Contemporary Christian music expert Tony Cummings, indicated that the average Christian contemporary album sold two and a half thousand copied during this period (cited in Ward, 2005:76). The fact that sales of *Signs of Change* were of the same general order would appear to indicate that those who bought the album were largely converted evangelical youth. The aspiration to connect with a secular constituency through their record was not realised. In some ways, this was not surprising. The release of *Signs of Change* coincided with the punk revolution which made prog rock look distinctly old fashioned. This was not something of which the band was unaware and the album effectively marked the end of After the Fire as a prog rock band (Carr, 1999:chapter 12). The group was soon to re-emerge with a more contemporary, hi-energy techno-pop sound and to be more successful (Scott, 2003:7).

In contrast to the views of social historians like Martin, Segrave, Cloonan and Street, this chapter has shown that Christians were not uniformly opposed to rock music, as it first emerged and developed at the end of the 1960s and early 1970s. It has also shown that evangelicals had a number of reasons for taking their rock music into the world. Young Christians were inspired by the tradition of gospel blues, the rock star and the vision of being salt and light in the world. It is possible that the reluctance of the church to use rock music in its own environs was a contributory factor in this move to the world. But if so, it was not of such an order as to occupy an important place in the reasoning of those who took their music to secular venues. What motivated young Christians was not an experience of exclusion but a sense of vocation.

5

The Discontents

This study has shown that the church was more willing to engage with 1960s youth music than social historians, such as Linda Martin, Kerry Segrave, Martin Cloonan and John Street, have suggested. There was not a default position of unremitting Christian opposition to the musical revolution of the period. That there were critical voices is hardly a matter of debate and has already been alluded too. This chapter takes a closer look at the reasons critics gave for their opposition to certain types of youth music and its use by the church. This theme will be explored through Charles Cleall's book *Music and Holiness,* which was the most sustained critique of the churches use of youth music during the 1960s. It will be supplemented by related material from the *Church Times,* the *Methodist Recorder,* the *Christian Herald* and *New Christian.* In terms of the overall argument of the study, that Martin, Segrave, Cloonan and Street exaggerate the extent of Christian opposition to 1960s youth music, it will also show that the critics themselves were criticised and that their views were far from universally accepted. As part of the same thesis, I begin by noticing the context which motivated a significant amount of the oppositional comment.

Beatlemania in the Church

During the 1960s, the *Methodist Recorder* regularly included a feature entitled 'Margaret Harwood's Postbag'. It was a 'problem page' type piece, in which men and women shared their concerns in the hope of wise advice. In an August issue of 1964, a letter from a Mrs L. A. from Leicester and the reply by Margaret Harwood express a shared loathing of the Beatles. The former, is critical of the Beatles' singing, their 'untidy unkempt hair' and their 'dirty shoes' (Harwood, *Methodist Recorder*, 13 August 1964:11). How Mrs L.A. had noticed the condition of the Beatles' shoes is not mentioned but she received a sympathetic reply from Harwood. Indeed, her comments were if anything more hostile. She compared the Beatles' music to that of 'several cats on the tiles', referred to their popularity as 'an adulation of the primitive' and complained that 'entertainment, so called, of this kind, is paid so highly, while serious work so often is not' (Harwood, Methodist Recorder, 13 August 1964:11). The comments of the correspondent and the 'agony aunt' reveal a deep antipathy towards the new musical trend. But what is significant is the pressure both ladies felt to think differently. In fact, this was the reason for Mrs L.A. from Leicester's letter. 'I'm told I must like the Beatles' she said, but found it impossible to do so and wondered what to do (Harwood, *Methodist Recorder*, 13 August 1964:11). Harwood testified to exactly the same experience and advised Mrs L.A. to be true to herself despite the clamour of support for the Beatles. Unfortunately, neither of the women identified where the pressure was coming from to embrace the new musical phenomenon. Given the enormous popularity of the Beatles and the largely positive way in which they were received, it is safe to conclude that much of it arose from popular culture. However, it would be unwise to exclude a sense of pressure arising from their church connections. Both Harwood and Mrs L.A. from Leicester were obviously very religious women and church was clearly central to their lives. It is quite likely that they sensed a pressure to like the Beatles from this direction also. Indeed, as readers of the *Methodist Recorder*, they would have been aware of the attention that the Beatles, beat music and its use in church had received within its pages in recent months. Just a few weeks before their correspondence was printed for example, the headline on the front page of the newspaper read 'Church with a beat' and featured an account of experimental worship with beat sounds (*Methodist Recorder*, 11 June 1964:1). This report, as with other references to beat music in worship during this period was largely positive. It seems likely that Mrs L.A. and Harwood felt pressure from within the church to like the Beatles and to endorse their style of music for use within congregational worship.

The perception of support for the Beatles and their type of pop within the church was a source of great concern for those who did not have any enthusiasm for this kind of youth music. Indeed, compared to other forms of youth music, beat music had the most potential to radically affect church worship during the decade. Folk music was well received by Christians and not generally regarded as contentious. Christian rock music emerged late in the decade and at this stage involved few young people and did not find its way into church worship until very much later. The emergence of beat music on the other hand, as the growth of beat services made clear, posed a challenge to the status quo. It is this sense of danger to tradition that best explains the amount of oppositional material to be found in the church press during the period of the beat boom. Over the entire decade, the volume of comment about youth music, critical or positive, was not large, but a significant proportion is to be found during the years of the beat boom. This is best illustrated by the *Methodist Recorder*, where from December 1963 to June 1964, there was what amounted to an ongoing debate about the merits of beat music. During this period not a month passed without some reference to the issue. This concentration of material is reflected in this chapter by the fact that roughly fifty per cent of quoted critical opinion comes from the period between 1963 and 1965. Traditionalists were motivated to act because they sensed that not only was pop music taking over the world, but it was also beginning to exert influence in the church.

The popularity of beat music in the church, not only explains the volume of criticism during this period, but also on occasion, its extreme rhetoric. The comments of Harwood above for example, illustrate the point. But this kind of language is perhaps best demonstrated by Charles Cleall in his book *Music and Holiness*. Published at the height of Beatlemania in 1964, it was supposed to be part of an 'enquiry' into a biblical theology of culture (Cleall, 1964:dust jacket). Instead of reasoned detachment that might be expected to characterise such a work however, it was a work of immense feeling and passion. In a 1965 review, the musical author, Rosemary Hughes, felt that this detracted from the value of *Music and Holiness* and that it had prompted the author to over simplify and overstate his arguments (Hughes, 1965:863). For example, after setting out his case against pop music in the second chapter of *Music and Holiness*, he concluded with the following assessment of its Christian use: 'In the home, it is deplorable; meriting tears. In the Church, it is a scandal; a stumbling block; a pollution: an intolerable blasphemy.' (Cleall, 1964:71). Such an uninhibited statement reflected a context in which traditionalists felt themselves to be under increasing pressure to give way to pop music.

It is possible that perceptions regarding the increasing popularity of pop music in the church, to the extent of even threatening traditional forms of worship, were inaccurate. The heightened sensitivities of those whose musical taste was not in sympathy with the Beatles' music might have encouraged an exaggeration of the problem. It is equally possible of course, that their assessments were more or less accurate. But allowing for a degree of over statement regarding the churches turn to pop, it cannot be reduced to the level imagined by Martin, Segrave, Cloonan and Street. On their scenario, there would be no perception of a church being taken over by pop music because the majority would be opposed to it. The sense of disquiet regarding pop's popularity within the church, emanating from critics like Cleall, cannot be discounted.

Cleall was a gifted musician, who was playing organ at Ashford Methodist Church by the time of his fourteenth birthday. There followed a career in music, which involved amongst other things, appointment to the teaching staff of Westminster Abbey, organist at Wesley's Chapel, London, conductor of the Glasgow Choral Union and Northern Divisional music specialist of Her Majesty's Inspectorate of Schools in Scotland. His research into the natural pitch of the human voice resulted in the common use of lower keys in new church hymnals (Charles Cleall, correspondence, 19 August 2006). Throughout, he remained a Methodist and *Music and Holiness* was published by Epworth press, the publishing arm of the Methodist Church. It was a systematic rejection of all modern pop sounds and its suitability for use in Christian worship. It cogently documented the case of those who were ill at ease with the new musical developments. Those concerns will now be explored.

Inferiority

Music and Holiness was profoundly shaped by a particular understanding of holiness. Understood as the kind of life acceptable to God, it has been variously interpreted by Christians over the years. These have frequently been motivated by the conviction, reflected in Jesus expectation that his disciples would be 'light' and 'salt' for example, that Christians should be distinctive in their attitudes and behaviour. For Charles Cleall, this meant that there must be no compromise with the world and the sinful nature of human kind. His exposition of this theme had some radical implications for music.

No Compromise

One of the most controversial applications of Cleall's views regarding holiness and music was what constituted the latter. Only that which reflected a 'remembrance of the divine' was properly to be termed music (Cleall, 1964:77-78). This meant that it should induce right moral feeling, educate the soul in virtue and be associated with purity and moral cleanliness. Such music was not only holy, but according to Cleall, also beautiful (Cleall, 1964:28ff). He contended:

> There exists in the Bible the concept that a thing is beautiful in so far as it is holy; that a work of art possesses aesthetic merit in so far as we meet in it, and know that we meet in it the Divine.
>
> (Cleall, 1964:31)

The implications for what Cleall variously described as pops, swing, rock 'n' roll and jazz, (he was not interested in distinguishing between them), was clear enough. They lacked aesthetic merit because they were not grounded in a 'remembrance of the divine' (Cleall, 1964:31). On the contrary, they were associated with 'savagery, seduction, perversion, cruelty' and debauchery (Cleall, 1964:61). Specifically, these included unacceptable films, degenerate youth, sexual immorality and even the origin of modern sounds. In a passage which reflected a sense of colonial superiority and racism, Jazz music is condemned because it was connected with supposed Negro ignorance and decadence. Negro spirituals were affirmed, but only because they are said to have escaped a background of barbarism and reaped the rewards of being influenced by European Christian civilisation (Cleall, 1964:45-46).

Also included on the list of pop's morally dubious associations was its connection with commercialism and the world of entertainment. Cleall refers to the words of Paul Johnson, assistant editor of *New Statesman*, which had suggested that pop was part of a 'commercial machine' which had 'enslaved' a generation of young people (Cleall, 1964:65). Such links were serious enough, but Cleall is appalled that commercial attitudes had found their way into the church with what he considered were profound moral implications. Quoting approvingly from the Dean of Lincoln, he suggested that the motive to increase the size of congregations involved priests in taking upon themselves the 'anxious concern of the theatre manager whose box office receipts are dwindling' (Cleall, 1964:53). The danger was that worship became entertainment, centred on the need to please human beings rather than God. To lose this 'essential God-centredness' involved a failure to obey the first commandment to love God and inevitably courted moral disaster (Cleall, 1964:43ff, 53). Such convictions, illustrated that Cleall's sense of the inferiority of the new music, was grounded not so much in its perceived lack of musical quality but by a particular moral sensibility. He certainly did not exclude comments on pop's musical shortcomings. This is evident for example, when he considered the use of the musical voice. The western classic tradition celebrated the idea of the trained voice, in contrast to the natural voice and the sometimes inarticulate groans and moans of pop and rock music. Unsurprisingly, Cleall mustered arguments in favour of the former. But even here the moral dimension is not lost. He suggested:

> The best pronunciation probably derives from considerateness toward our fellows: it is a sympathetic, kindly way of approach; a sign of good manners, which rougher forms of speech cannot indicate.
>
> (Cleall, 1964:47)

Here, as elsewhere, Cleall's belief in the inferiority of electric youth music is centred upon his understanding of holiness. Pop was not worthy because of its many immoral associations, if used in worship it reflected a diversion from the church's central task and in its forms of speech lacked common civility.

Guilty by Association

Not all of Cleall's themes were welcomed with the same degree of enthusiasm by concerned Christians. His interest in pop vocal styles for example, does not appear to have caused much grievance elsewhere. But there was comment on youth music's perceived link with impropriety. The Reverend Dr F. B. West-brook for example, a prominent member of the Methodist Church Music Society, reviewed *Music and Holiness* in the *Methodist Recorder* and gave it his unequivocal support. He posed the question:

> Is this type of melody, harmony and rhythm, which had its origin in the night club, the tap room and the dance hall, able adequately to express a pure and unsullied worship?
>
> (Westbrook, *Methodist Recorder*, 21 January 1965:9)

The answer to the question was never in doubt. He maintained that Cleall's book was a 'Courageous and well informed attempt to make clear to all who worship that we do not honour God or serve him aright by compromising spiritual and artistic standards' (Westbrook, *Methodist Recorder*, 21 January 1965:9). Similar convictions were expressed by others. Earlier, I drew attention to Edward H. Patey's description of an experimental act of worship in Liverpool; his account included some vociferous responses to the televised service, one of which began:

> Disgusted, disgusted, disgusted with the programme you had on television on Christmas Eve. To think of a most beautiful Cathedral brought down to these depths, a programme suitable only for the Cavern.
>
> (Patey, *New Christian*, 08 February 1968:4)

While another complained to a local Liverpudlian newspaper:

> The beauty and dignity, even popularity of Liverpool Cathedral are not enhanced by beat music rendered by youths badly in need of a hair cut. The sonorous tones of the great organ, playing music by Brahms, Schubert and Mendelssohn are what people of good taste and Christian sentiment want and expect.
>
> (Patey, *New Christian*, 08 February 1968:4)

A sense of outrage clearly permeated both of these letters and its source appears to echo the concerns of Charles Cleall. The holy beauty of the Christian sanctuary seemed incongruous with 'youths badly in need of a hair cut' and music which reflected a pop venue like the Cavern.

Cleall's concern about the commercial nature of youth music was also taken up by others. His criticism of commercial attitudes within the church, pandering to youth when its worship should have focussed on God, took an interesting turn in the *Christian Herald*. The growing use of contemporary music in reader's churches prompted an ongoing discussion on the letters page during the latter part of 1969 and early 1970. The relative lateness of this correspondence, (Methodists and Anglicans had discussed the issues six years previously), probably reflects the strongly conservative nature of the *Herald's* readership. Something of the evangelistic bias of the *Herald* can be also seen in that it bannered the correspondence 'Convert – not entertain', where as Cleall had criticised pop music because it diverted the church from its proper task of worship. An early letter was from R. Dingwall of Ross-shire who expressed the concern precisely: 'The aim of the Church should be conversion – not entertainment – for the young' (Dingwall, *Christian Herald*, 01 December 1969:361). The 13 December issue of the *Christian Herald* included two responses which challenged the assertion that the Christian use of pop music was merely providing entertainment for youth. One of these, from a Mrs I. C. Hastings, testified to the way in which a local gang leader and his friends had been converted by going to see a Christian pop group. The letter concluded: 'Someone has to reach these people. One has to forget self, likes and dislikes' (Hastings, *Christian Herald*, 13 December 1969:489). This did not appear to be the view of the *Christian Herald's* leadership however. In February 1970, the concluding letter of the series was given prominence at the top of the letters page and headed 'Message for youth'. The correspondent, an Albert Fisher from Hove, referred to the increasing amount of pop in church and connected this with entertainment for the young. Like others before him, he noticed in passing some of the questionable associations of youth music and contrasted this with God's call to holiness. But in his concluding and climactic appeal he reminded youngsters of the true purpose of worship:

> Young people, enjoy your 'pop' records if you must, your games, your social activities; but when you enter the doors of a church, remember that you are there to bow down in reverence, and to worship God in spirit, and acknowledge Him as Supreme. If you can really achieve this, you will become aware that there is no dullness; and you will wonder why you never saw it before.
>
> (Fisher, *Christian Herald*, 14 February 1970:137)

As well as a perception that commercialism was growing within the church and that this involved an improper focus on entertainment, there were those like the prominent Methodist, Donald Soper, who were critical of youth music because of its connection to commercial culture itself. This understanding probably had its roots in the political theory of Theodor Adorno.

Adorno was the most sophisticated thinker of what came to be called the 'Frankfurt School' of neo-Marxist theorists. Founded in 1923, this group was attached to the University of Frankfurt and attacked popular capitalist culture (Shuker, 1994:22). Adorno himself focused on music and his first essay on the subject was published in 1941. He argued that in capitalist societies the need to make a profit entailed the mass production of music, not unlike the processes involved in the manufacture of other items. The main effect of this was a kind of standardisation, typical of the industrial process. Certain music might appear novel, but the reality was the endless repetition of certain musical formulae (Adorno, 1990:301ff). Noticing its mass appeal, he focused upon the theme of 'distraction', by which attention to popular music prevented individuals from perceiving their true condition and dissipated their potential for challenging the status quo (Adorno, 1990:314). Adorno's disparaging view of popular music and its responsibility for blinding the masses of their need of social transformation, bequeathed a loathing of popular music in left wing circles. It is likely that they provided the background to Soper's comments in the *Methodist Recorder* in March 1964 in which he criticised the Beatles.

Soper's socialist sympathies were well known, in the *Recorder* article he appeared to express a preference for living in the Soviet Union rather than capitalist Britain (Soper, *Methodist Recorder*, 05 March 1964:2). The catalyst for this extraordinary statement was the Beatles' success. Their elevation revealed that society had 'lost its way' and was preoccupied with 'trivial and evanescent' pop music when its most urgent need was to develop true spiritual and political beliefs (Soper, *Methodist Recorder*, 05 March 1964:2). Although refracted through a Christian lens, Soper's comments echo Adorno's theme of distraction and there can be no doubt about his scepticism regarding the worth of the Beatles' music:

> It is nothing short of comic to hear musicians, who should know better, talking about the musical novelty and uniqueness of the Liverpool sound, as if three guitars and an assortment of drums have suddenly created a new rhythmic genre. What balderdash!
> (Soper, *Methodist Recorder*, 05 March 1964:2)

At the height of his rhetoric he asks: 'Is there among it all one memorable chord, one inventive piece of counterpart, one creative melodic line? There is not.' (Soper, *Methodist Recorder*, 05 March 1964:2). Not all of pop music's critics will have shared Soper's politics, but his sharp edged pen undoubtedly expressed what others felt, that it was an inferior music unworthy of Christian use, largely because of its perceived connections with the unholy.

Addiction

Cleall was not unaware of the appeal of modern music to the young. But for him this was part of the problem. In *Music and Holiness,* he listed nineteen words that were used to describe modern sounds. These included adjectives such as 'alluring', 'captivating, 'enchanting' and 'ravishing'. He then located the root of each adjective and finally isolated the meaning (Cleall, 1964:54). So for the four examples above, the following pattern resulted:

We call things	but the root of	
We greatly like	that word is	which means
Alluring	loire	bait, as of a trap
Captivating	capere	to take prisoner
Enchanting	incantare	to bind with a spell
Ravishing	rapere	to seize by force.
		(Cleall, 1964:54)

For Cleall, it was the core meaning of the words that was significant. They indicated that youth music could bring about a dangerous kind of addiction from which it was difficult to break free.

'Into the Groove'

The explanation of pop music's dangerous power to enslave was, according to Cleall, that it stimulated extraordinarily powerful instincts and sensual desires acting below the surface of conscious mind (Cleall, 1964:54-57). Similar to the experience of falling in love, one might be overtaken by such music in a way that was 'immediate, unthinking and involuntary' (Cleall, 1964:55, 87). It is possible that Cleall might have had in mind some of the exuberant reactions to early rock 'n' roll. There is every possibility that he was re-flecting upon the growing Beatlemania of the period. Cer-tainly, the presentation of youth music as addictive by virtue of its appeal to the senses, offered an excellent perspective from which to question the validity of its use in church. Its basis in pleasure and sensual appetite was interpreted as al-together unworthy (Cleall, 1964:39, 57). It contrasted sharply with true church music which gave no quarter to sen-sation and appealed to the mind rather than the body (Cleall, 1964:85ff). According to Cleall plainsong was the ideal, be-cause it was:

> Superlatively contrived never to 'get into the groove'; never to become 'fast bound in sin and nature's night'; never to become the minion of the unconscious mind, or the demonic powers which war with the Holy Spirit for the soul of man.
>
> (Cleall, 1964:93)

Youth music of course, was reckoned to do all of these things by the route of sensuous delight. Its ability to overwhelm and take over a young person's life was dangerous for two reasons. On the one hand, it raised the spectre of idolatry and placed something other than God at the centre of ones life, while it also posed a threat to human dignity by removing freedom and the capacity to be a free agent (Cleall, 1964:56ff). Yet in develop-ing these arguments, Cleall's concern was not so much with those, who he regarded, were the victims of pop outside the church, but with those who were addicted within it. Conse-quently, the concern about idolatry had a peculiarly ecclesial bias. Cleall complained that by using beat music church leaders themselves were guilty of this sin. Their use of youth music was said to reveal that they were more concerned with pleasing the crowds than with pleasing God (Cleall, 1964:34ff). He declared:

> To delight in anything other *but* sanctity is idolatry. To seek to please man in our worship is to turn the House of Prayer into a den

of thieves; because we steal from God His sovereignty for our own aggrandizement.

(Cleall, 1964:37)

For Cleall, worship was not to be connected with any missionary minded attempts to win the unconverted, 'Nothing in our worship should be there as a sop or bait to man' he stated (Cleall, 1964:37). Congregational praise needed no justification beyond itself. But in order to worship the holy, holy music was necessary and this did not include addictive youth music, whose appeal was located in base human instincts and pleasures.

'Turn it down a bit!'

Cleall's concern about the addictive nature of youth music was reflected in the Christian press during the 1960s. There does not appear to have been a great deal of comment about where Cleall located its power to attract, or the idolatry of Christians in using such music in church, but criticism can be found of young people for their exuberance. It was noted above, that Cleall's comments about the addictive nature of modern music was likely to have been prompted by the Beatlemania of the period. But Christian concern about the extent of young people's passion and enthusiasm for their music began before that time. In September 1969, the Reverend Gavin Reid, a prominent Evangelical, who later became the Bishop of Maidstone, wrote an article for the *Christian Herald*. He described some of the enormous cultural changes that had occurred in recent times and discussed the implications for Christian work among young people. In the course of this article, he described the changing musical scene and his own attitudes towards this. By 1969, he had come to have a very liberal attitude and acknowledged the legitimate use of pop music in a Christian context. But at the beginning of the decade he admitted to a very different approach. At that time he considered that the pop industry had begun to 'exercise a tyrannical reign over

young people' (Reid, *Christian Herald*, 13 September 1969:210).
He banned record players from the church hall because he felt it
had 'unhealthily got out of all proportion, and was having a
drug-like effect on some' (Reid, *Christian Herald*, 13 September
1969:210).

Concerns about the 'drug-like effect' of pop music on
young people undoubtedly grew as the Beatles emerged. In
the Christian press, evidence of this can be seen in the words
of the Reverend Reginald Bedford, the National Secretary of
the Methodist Association of Youth Clubs (MAYC). As the
figurehead of MAYC, he frequently addressed his young audience through the youth page in the *Methodist Recorder*. In
December 1963, as Beatlemania was getting under way he
wrote an open letter to fans of the group. The subject of Bedford's correspondence was almost entirely devoted to the
theme of enthusiasm and of the sort that was generated by
the Beatles. Initially, he is mildly approving, comparing the
passion surrounding the music with his own love of soccer.
'There is no need to apologise for getting excited about the
Beatles' he suggested (Bedford, *Methodist Recorder*, 26 December 1963:8). However, even in this part of the article
there is some ambivalence, in a reference to the long queues
for tickets to see the group he observed: 'Mind you, if everybody would stay at home until the morning, they would all
get tickets and a night's sleep as well' (Bedford, *Methodist
Recorder*, 26 December 1963:8). In the latter part of the letter this gentle reprove gives way to scorn of the 'mass hysteria' which surrounded the group. Noticing that girls were the
'worse offenders', he offered some practical reasons why this
was inappropriate behaviour. Screaming had made some live
performances impossible and the Beatles were ordinary young
people like his readers. But Bedford is primarily concerned
with two other consequences of allowing the Beatles to become the subject of an all consuming passion. In the first
place, as Cleall was later to do, he warned about the danger
to human freedom and dignity:

Once you get the mass hysteria started, you can do almost what you like. Don't be hoodwinked. You too, can be a prisoner caught up with all the rest – shouting, screaming, and worshipping.

(Bedford, *Methodist Recorder*, 26 December 1963:8)

The reference to 'worshipping', naturally leads into the other main area of Bedford's concern, which focussed on spirituality. This not only included the danger of idolatry but also ignoring social need:

If you're not careful the 'Mersey Sound' will stop you hearing other important things like the cries of hungry people asking, not for a Beatle to shake his head, but for food to make life possible. If you keep on worshipping false gods, you may even miss the call of the One who said, 'Follow me.'

(Bedford, *Methodist Recorder*, 26 December 1963:8)

In conclusion, Bedford advised his young readers 'Good Beatling! But turn it down a bit!' (Bedford, *Methodist Recorder*, 26 December 1963:8).

Bedford's letter prompted a number of responses in following editions of the *Methodist Recorder*. The Reverend Fred Milson, senior lecturer and head of the Youth and Community Service Department at Westhill Training College, Selly Oak, complained that it was 'about as paternalistic and patronising a piece that that was ever penned for Methodist teenagers'. But no other letters were printed which supported this view. In his letter, Milson had questioned whether the youth page really was for the young people of Methodism, or whether it was dedicated to 'what older Methodists think ought to be said to younger Methodists (Milson, *Methodist Recorder*, 09 January 1964:14). The lack of published material from ordinary young people opposing Bedford's point of view, might suggest that it was a pertinent question. Of course, it may have been the case that there were no letters supporting Milson against Bedford. But what was printed certainly upheld the authority of the head of MAYC. In the final piece of correspondence upon this issue, the youth page even called upon the Reverend Frank Cumbers, a well respected establishment figure, to give an adult view. He considered that Bedford had spoken 'admirably' (Cumbers, *Methodist Recorder*, 06 February 1964:14).

Harm

An addiction to drugs or alcohol usually produces harmful consequences. When commentators used the image of stimulants to describe the captivating potential of pop music, it was not surprising that they should go on to discuss the practical harm this might cause. In what follows, I will show how a number of Christians developed this theme, before returning to *Music and Holiness* to consider how Charles Cleall regarded the injurious nature of pop music.

Side Effects

Reference has already been made to the dangerous consequences that Reginald Bedford associated with an improper devotion to the Beatles. But in addressing a general concern about the threat to human freedom and dignity he offered the allusive comment, mainly aimed at young girls, that once affected by the hysteria 'you can almost do what you like' (Bedford, *Methodist Recorder*, 26 December 1963:8). Such a general statement might well have had a wide application. But there is every possibility that it included the expression of what was regarded as inappropriate sexual feelings and behaviour. Earlier in his article Bedford had located the source of Beatlemania at exactly this point. Addressing girls, since they were the 'worst offenders' when it came to the passion surrounding the Beatles, he explained: 'And – let's be frank – it's because they get you worked up in a sexy sort of way you can't explain (Bedford, *Methodist Recorder*, 26 December 1963:8). If Bedford provided a mild hint of pop music's association with sexual impropriety, the comments of a young correspondent, who supported Bedford's stance on Beatlemania, provided an alternative link between the addictive nature of pop music and other problems in society:

> I agree with him that it is about time that teenagers (myself included) realised that there is more to life than the Beatles and pop music. I admit, much as I like the Beatles music myself, some of the teenagers who go to their shows get carried away too much, and then take the law into their own hands and cause a lot of trouble.
>
> (*Methodist Recorder*, 23 January 1964:14)

This use of the image of addiction to explain pop music's capacity to inspire lawless behaviour can also be seen elsewhere. The Reverend C. Champneys Burnham from Hastings provides a notable example. Writing in his parish magazine, he blamed beat music for the disturbances between 'mods' and 'rockers' during the August bank holiday of 1964 (*Church Times*, 21 August 1964:9). The mechanism by which this was thought to happen appeared to revolve around the notion, that just like drugs, beat music produced behaviours which were unacceptable. According to Burnham, pop sounds produced a kind of 'madness' which affected the 'minds and conduct of many youngsters who without it would be perfectly normal' (*Church Times*, 21 August 1964:9). He went on:

> It intoxicates them more effectively than would alcohol, and it inflames and distorts their emotions in as deadly a fashion as drugs. I am dead against it and regard it as one of the greatest evils of the age.
>
> (*Church Times*, 21 August 1964:9)

Such strong oppositional statements were clearly felt to be newsworthy by the *Church Times* who published Burnham's comments. They would undoubtedly have been approved by Charles Cleall.

Trance and Propelling Force

In attempting to show the adverse impact of pop music, Cleall drew attention to what he perceived to be two effects of the powerful beat of this kind of music. The first of these concerned the tendency of the beat to encourage trance like states, the other suggested that it had a tendency to propel young people towards certain immoral behaviours. The idea of trance and sending force might be seen as a further extension of the music as drug analogy, since both were associated with certain types of narcotic. But this is not something that Cleall pursued with any enthusiasm, preferring instead to use certain expert witnesses to prosecute his case against pop music. One of these witnesses was Dr Ian Oswald, Beit Memorial Research Fellow at the Institute of Experimental Psychology at the University of Oxford, who had researched the nature of loud rhythmic music upon the body. Quoting Oswald, Cleall explained at some length how this type of music resulted in reduced blood flow to the brain and impaired consciousness (Cleall, 1964:59). This in itself was said to produce moral effects reducing the ability for reflective thought (Cleall, 1964:60). But perhaps the most powerful suggestion was that the trance like state engendered by beat music enabled evil to penetrate the mind. In its weakened condition, the mind was said to be susceptible to the immoral content of modern songs, which might come to control thought and dictate behaviour (Cleall, 1964:63). In the pursuance of this argument, Cleall called upon another expert witness, the prominent Methodist scholar, Dr Leslie Weatherhead. In his book *Psychology, Religion and Healing*, Weatherhead had suggested that the New Testament phenomena of demon possession might be understood, in a twentieth century context, as having to do with the domination of the unconscious mind by evil thoughts. Cleall took up this idea to indicate that pop music might be one of the means by which this occurred. He offered the suggestion that 'lascivious songs introduce demons into man's heart' and was consequently responsible for all kinds of evil, including adultery, murder, theft and blasphemy (Cleall, 1964:63).

The other key strand in Cleall's attack upon pop music as a source of harm, centred upon the notion that beat was a kind of driving force which propelled young people to sexual immorality. In developing this theme, he referred to an article written by the educationist and Fellow of King's College, Cambridge, David Holbrook, which had appeared in the *New Statesmen and Nation* in March 1964. Cleall agreed with Holbrook that the beat of modern pop was 'a kind of sending movement', which drove young people to satisfy their sexual desires (Cleall, 1964:68). For Cleall, rhythm and blues was seen as the ultimate expression of sexual music, which when combined with the performance of the artist, (which following Holbrook, he can present as 'a dissipated sexual act'), was thought to be considerable. It was an encouragement to sexual adventure, a threat to chastity and responsible for the spread of venereal disease (Cleall, 1964:60-61, 68-69).

The extensive and detailed nature of Cleall's critique of modern pop music was unequalled in British churches during the 1960s. In subsequent years, he was to change his mind about the matters on which he had pronounced so strongly and considered some of his attitudes of the time to be 'rigid' (Charles Cleall interview, 24.04.07). Yet, as I have shown, there were plenty of others who were prepared to voice their concerns about pop music and to complain of its use by the church. However, such views did not go unchallenged.

Pop Strikes Back

The correspondents of the *Christian Herald* who challenged the assertion that pop music in church was merely a cheap gimmick designed to entertain young people, was just one of a number of examples where the supporters of youth music gave expression to their opinion. The experimental act of worship in Liverpool Cathedral devised by Edward H. Patey had its critics, as was noted earlier. But Patey revealed that the letters of appreciation outnumbered the letters of criticism. He viewed this as significant given that 'protestors normally put pen to paper more quickly than appreciators' (Patey, *New Christian*, 08 February 1968:2). The affirmation of pop music in the face of controversy was not an isolated phenomenon. In this section, I will show how the Christian supporters of pop music challenged the views of critics that it was a harmful influence, unsuitable as a vehicle of worship and outreach and that it was an entirely inferior form of music.

Positive effects

One of the most noteworthy reactions to criticism of pop music was the response to Dr Donald Soper's outspoken comments in the *Methodist Recorder*. As was observed earlier, in March 1964 Soper made a number of derogatory comments about the Beatles' music. Two weeks later, the newspaper printed ten letters of reply, only one of which was supportive. Correspondents attacked different aspects of Soper's article, not all of which were directly related to the Beatles and beat music. His preference for life in the Soviet Union for example, was the focus of concern for a couple of correspondents. Of the remaining seven, one was concerned that Soper's 'vicious attacks' might dissuade young people from having any association with the church. Four letters criticised Soper's opinion of the Beatles, while the remaining two suggested that beat music had a place in the churches work with young people and indeed its worship (*Methodist Recorder*, 19 March 1964:2). Of those who wrote in direct support of the Beatles, the theme of their influence on the lives of young people was prominent. Interestingly, this was not a major feature of Soper's article, although he clearly thought the Beatles were not a force for good within society. He accused the group of unconsciously pandering to 'a dangerous eruption of early puberty sexual feelings' and regarded the hysteria which surrounded them as a 'rootless substitute' for the truly 'full life'. Nevertheless, he did not stress beat music's harmful effects as others had done and were to do (Soper, *Methodist Recorder*, 05 March 1964:2). That replies to Soper's article which directly supported the Beatles, tended to focus on this issue, probably reflected the sensitivity of this topic within the church at the time. One of the correspondents who opposed Soper, a Mrs Myrtle Fox from Bromley in Kent, gives a sense of how Beatle's supporters couched their arguments:

> I am middle aged, and a school teacher and I can see that these boys are an influence for good in many respects, and at least they are clean and so are their songs. Already they have helped not only their country, but their own district, and their own streets.
>
> (Fox, *Methodist Recorder*, 19 March 1964:2)

The impact of the Beatles and the beat boom on 'their own streets' was also taken up by a K. Bray from Cardiff:

> Dr Soper criticises the effect of the Beatles on the lives of young people today. I would like to know how he consolidates this view with the fact that teenage crime in Liverpool has declined noticeably with the rise of the very many Merseyside Beat groups.
>
> (Bray, *Methodist Recorder*, 19 March 1964:2)

In contrast to those who maintained that pop and beat did harm, there were those as this correspondence reveals, who were prepared to argue an alternative case.

Place in the Church

The letters in the Methodist Recorder on 19 March 1964 also touched on beat music's place in evangelism and worship. Again, this was not a prominent aspect of Soper's article. Almost in passing he mentioned that the Salvation Army was investing in guitars and 'Mersey beat' and implied that this was not likely to be a successful venture (Soper, *Methodist Recorder*, 05 March 1964:2). That this reference was followed up by correspondents, again suggests that it was a very relevant issue for the Methodist Church at the time. Of the two letters which mention Soper's reference to the Salvation Army and its use of pop and beat, the lengthiest came from a Charles Wield of Harrow who considered the attack on the Salvation Army 'cheap and unworthy' (Laurie, *Methodist Recorder*, 19 March 1964:2). He contradicted Soper's suggestion that their strategy of using youth music was unsuccessful and indicated that 'scores of similar groups' were operating in Methodist youth clubs and that some had been involved in Methodist worship. But perhaps the most interesting letter on this subject came some weeks later from the Reverend Morgan Rees, a Methodist minister working in Durham. The piece was given particular prominence in the letters section of the *Recorder* and was headlined 'Salvation Army and Mersey Beat' (Rees, *Methodist Recorder*, 09 April 1964:5). Rees shared much of Soper's analysis of beat music and regarded it as 'distasteful'. However, he believed that the Salvation Army might be right in adopting 'Mersey Beat' and argued that its appropriation by Christians might have enormous evangelistic possibilities. He compared the use of youth music to John Wesley's decision to preach in the open air. Wesley had not found the prospect appealing and wrote in his journal that it meant 'submitting to be more vile', Rees asked whether the modern church needed to be ready 'to be more vile' by being prepared to use beat music (Rees, *Methodist Recorder*, 09 April 1964:5). He continued:

> It is not that I could imagine myself playing an electric guitar, but I am quite prepared to let others do it, if by such means the way is prepared for the proclaiming of Christ. 'I am become all things to all men' says St Paul, 'that I may by all means save some' (1 Corinthians, 9:22). It needs but a spark of God's grace and there

could be a mighty conflagration – a whole generation won for Christ and the greatest religious revival of our time.

(Rees, *Methodist Recorder*, 09 April 1964:5)

Such expectations of beat music was unusual among its Christian supporters, that they should be expressed by one who regarded it as 'distasteful' was extraordinary. Beyond its inflated assessment of what God could achieve through music, its significance is to be found in the willingness of Rees to use youth music even though he had no enthusiasm for it. The prominent placing of Rees' letter in the *Recorder* may suggest that this was not an uncommon view, it certainly seems to indicate that it was an opinion the newspaper was happy to endorse. It is unlikely that Rees' pragmatic approach to the issue of the new music and its use by the church would have found favour with Soper, but it illustrates how even a dislike of beat and pop did not inevitably produce the kind of result critics would have desired. Even those who supported their view of youth music were not always prepared to endorse a ban on its use by the church.

Pop Value

Although the letters the *Methodist Recorder* printed in response to Dr Soper's attack on the Beatles reflected an overwhelming support for the group, only one correspondent seriously questioned Dr Soper's view that the Beatles' music lacked any kind of artistic merit or credibility. K. Bray from Cardiff wondered on what basis Soper had made his disparaging comments:

I was struck by Dr Soper's obvious lack of knowledge of any factual detail concerning 'pop' music. Never does he refer to an actual song sung by the Beatles, but instead refers rather vaguely to 'croaking accompaniments to childish shrieks.

(Bray, *Methodist Recorder*, 19 March 1964:2)

A growing sense that the critics were wrong to regard pop music as entirely worthless and inferior can also be observed in the pages of the *New Christian*.

When *New Christian* was first published in 1965, its own assessment of the musical taste of its readers can be gauged by the fact that in its review section, which commonly included analysis of books, television, theatre, cinema and science, there was also a regular feature on opera. Articles and reviews suggest that *New Christian* readers were likely to welcome new hymnody and (increasingly) folk music in church worship. There were affirming reports of new church song books like *Dunblane Praises, Hymns and Songs* and *100 Hymns for Today,* which contained both types of song (*New Christian,* 28 December 1967:4, 08 August 1968:20). The support for folk sounds was underlined by an article in which Sydney Carter articulated its relevance and usefulness for church worship (Carter, *New Christian,* 18 April 1968:9). Peter D. Smith's popular folk collection *Faith, Folk and Clarity* also received a favourable reception (Luff, *New Christian,* 28 November 1968:21). As far as pop sounds were concerned *New Christian* was inclined to be rather more ambivalent. One major reason for this was that contributors were influenced by the work of Richard Hoggart, and The Centre for Contemporary Cultural Studies in Birmingham, which he founded.

In 1957, Hoggart wrote a landmark book *The Uses of Literacy,* which while applauding the folk culture of working class people, criticised the shallowness of the mass entertainment industry in capitalist cultures (Cobb, 2005:53-54). Driven by the need for commercial success it was said to produce art of poor quality which lacked worthwhile values. After Theodor Adorno and the 'Frankfurt School' this was not a particularly remarkable left wing perspective, but unusually this was not where Hoggart's argument ended. He also maintained that with careful study popular culture could reveal important insights about the meaning of life. In October 1966, *New*

Christian produced a sympathetic report on the work of the Birmingham Centre and endorsed Hoggart's approach to popular culture. In relation to the pop scene, the author of the article Roger King argued:

> The system is corrupt, commercial, unconcerned with quality. Yes, all this. But at the same time, The Animals' *We Gotta Get Outta This Place* says more of what it means to be a teenager in England today than anything else. It might be nice if *The Blackleg Minor* or Mozart did: the point is, that they do not. Popular art is dealing with important areas of experience which so-called 'high' arts have ignored.
>
> (King, *New Christian,* 06 October 1966:8)

From this point onwards, *New Christian* began to take rather more interest in the world of youth music.

The following year saw the first appearance of a 'Popspot' column which was to appear erratically until the end of the paper's life. In one such column, Nicholas Fogg presented a general overview of the 1960s music scene, adopting a virtually identical perspective to King's:

> It is this ability to resist, albeit only just, the ferocious commercial pressures, which gives pop its life-line. At worst it is a banal reproduction of the lowest common denominator, tinkling like, and in exchange for, the money in your pocket; at best it is perhaps the sole honest attempt to create a poetry in an age when the contemporary high-brow is largely synonymous with meaningless obscurantism. Nowadays when I hear the word 'culture', I reach for my Beatles' 'Revolver' LP.
>
> (Fogg, *New Christian,* 07 March 1968:21)

Revolver had been the subject of an earlier review in *New Christian,* the author Peter Hardman, revealed once again the influence of Hoggart. Such is the Beatles achievement that they are now regarded as the purveyors of folk art:

It will be a great pity if the words of these songs are so drowned by the compelling beat of the music that their deep insight and profound comment on the human condition are obscured. In these songs the Beatles have given us authentic folk-songs of the mid-twentieth century, touching as they do upon the deepest human feelings and emotions in the context of a genuine idiom.

(Hardman, *New Christian*, 26 January 1967:20)

Two or three years earlier, at the time Soper and Cleall were making their criticisms, when the Beatles' musical and literary style was rather simpler, it is unlikely that Hardman would have been so effusive in his compliments. Yet the *New Christian* writers should be set apart from the more thorough going critics. Whilst acknowledging a bias towards inferiority and triviality, they also perceived that youth music could contain genuine insight and value, a possibility which seemed unlikely to those who wished the church to ignore and avoid the new music altogether.

This chapter has shown that parts of the 1960s church was strongly opposed to the Beatles and beat sounds. Indeed, I have unearthed comments which are as strong as anything social historians commonly quote to prove that the whole of the church was disengaged from popular culture and disinclined to change its musical traditions. But even amongst this concerned criticism there are clear indicators that the views of Martin, Segrave, Cloonan and Street exaggerate the situation in the church. The opposition occurred as a response to a perception that beat music was increasingly being accepted and used by congregations. Furthermore, the critic's arguments did not automatically hold sway. The claim that beat and pop was harmful, inappropriate for use by the church and inferior was opposed by those with more sympathetic views of modern music.

6

Decline

It is not inconceivable that the Christian appropriation of 1960s youth music might have initiated a trend in which pop, folk and rock music were increasingly used by the church. In this final chapter, it will be shown that in the following decades of the twentieth century this did not happen. I will describe the general decline of youth musical styles within the church and attempt to provide some explanation of it. For convenience, attention will be divided between Christian performance music, such as evangelical pop, rock and folk fusions of these which were largely located outside the church, and youth music which was used within the church as part of its worship. I begin with a discussion of evangelical performance music.

Performance

With groups like After the Fire to the fore, contemporary Christian music appeared to be in good health as the 1970s gave way to the 1980s. BBC radio and television took note of what appeared to be a growing phenomenon. In 1981 and 1982, Radio One presented live broadcasts from the Greenbelt festival. In 1984, BBC television aired the first series of *The Rock Gospel Show* which featured the talents of many evangelical musicians. The series usually attracted between two and three million viewers (Broadcasters Audience Research Board Report, 1984:April-June). This did not compare favourably with religious output of a more traditional kind; *Praise Be* for example, was watched by around five million viewers during this period. But the BBC proceeded to screen a further two series. It helped to give the impression that contemporary Christian music might make an impact beyond the boundaries of evangelical youth culture. In reality, the situation was far from healthy. One indication of this was the merging of Christian music production companies. After years of struggle, MGO became linked to the Christian publishers Kingsway in 1977, another Christian label, Chapel Lane, followed the same route in 1981. These difficulties were not mirrored in the United States of America where the Jesus music of the 1970s morphed into a multi-million dollar industry (Powell, 2003:10). Although British groups like Iona and Delirious would make distinctive musical contributions in the 1990s, it was America which provided the source of most contemporary Christian music (Powell, 2003:250-252, 436-437). Perhaps the greatest symbol of the declining situation in the United Kingdom was the condition of the Greenbelt festival. Although it recovered in the first years of the new millennium, the show case of Christian engagement with the arts, in which contemporary performance music was an important component, almost went out of business during the 1990s (Greenbelt Festival, 1999). Indeed, any account of concert orientated Christian youth music cannot be divorced from economic realities. The demise of Christian folk, pop and rock performance music is partly explained by its failure to generate a viable market for its music. This becomes especially clear when compared with the success of praise and worship music.

Economics

In his analysis of the changing shape of evangelical music during the 1970s and 1980s, Pete Ward argued that a key factor in the decline of Christian performance music was economic. He compared the financial returns of gospel artists with that of praise and worship. A crucial feature was the ability of the latter to develop multiple revenue streams via worship books, copyright income and recorded material (Ward, 2005:76ff). Album sales could also be generated in a variety of ways. Links could be made with branded collections of worship songs such as *Songs of Fellowship* or with special evangelical festivals like Spring Harvest. Revenue could also be developed through compilations of previously recorded material (Ward, 2005:78-9). In the limited evangelical musical market such varied streams of revenue were crucial to economic viability. In contrast, the typical folk, pop or rock artist provided few revenue sources beyond that of albums and concerts. Moreover, a comparison of album sales also served to underline the problems of performance music. This is illustrated by the amount of worship music sold at the Spring Harvest festival.

Spring Harvest began in 1979 as a training conference on evangelism and its popularity as a focus for teaching and worship grew rapidly during the 1980s. The event helped the spread of charismatic styles of worship across the country and in particular showcased the work of Graham Kendrick (Ward, 2005:71). Word Records sold one hundred thousand units linked to the festival between 1985 and 1989. The album connected to the Spring Harvest of 1989 sold twenty thousand copies (Ward, 2005:76). These figures dwarf those associated with Christian performance. The average sales of two and half thousand copies per album during the 1970s, was not much changed during the 1980s (Ward, 2005:76). These considerations, while highlighting the feasibility of praise and worship, revealed the poor financial returns from performance based Christian music. The market for evangelical folk, pop and rock performance music was not large enough to sustain a viable industry. The situation was not helped by the continually evolving secular music scene. The fusion of different musical genres, which was so central to the 1960s musical revolution, continued in the decades that followed. The youth music scene became increasingly fragmented. It meant that Christians concerned to imitate any one style were likely to find only limited support for their brand of music within the church. For artists, the impact of performance music's struggles was demoralising.

In 1979, Norman Miller was one of the leading promoters of Christian musicians and concerts. He candidly declared: 'Britain is just not big enough to support full-time gospel artists. Some of our artists are literally living on the bread line' (*Buzz*, January 1979:4). His comments were not inaccurate. In the early 1970s for example, John Russell, later to become a guitarist with After the Fire, played in the Christian band Narnia. But in 1975 he left, complaining:

> We were paying for ourselves to be in that band! Everyone thought that we all must have been well off – In fact we were all on the bread line, never knowing where the next gallon of petrol was coming from. Now I'd like to earn some money for being a musician, and feeling that I'm worth something. As it was you could work fifty-odd hours, up and down the motorway, just to get a fiver. It was ridiculous.
>
> (cited in Carr, 1999:chapter 7)

Before the release of the album *Signs of Change*, even After the Fire was struggling, as vocalist Andy Piercy explained:

> We can't afford to go forward because we need another investment of ten thousand pounds in lights and rig and truck. We can't afford to stop because we already have a debt of four and a half thousand pounds. It's like you reach the top of a hill and you're just about to go over and your back wheels start slipping.
>
> (cited in Carr, 1999:chapter 11)

In 1981, at a time when Christian music appeared to be flourishing, Kingsway Music produced a special brochure which was distributed through *Buzz* magazine. It was headed 'Something is seriously wrong with Christian music' and told of the financial plight of Christian artists (Kingsway Music, 1981).

Concern was expressed for those who were at the 'grass roots' and did not enjoy the 'limelight', yet an inspection of those who were needing support included established musicians such as Graham Kendrick, Ishmael and Iva Twydell. The brochure outlined a number of strategies to address this situation. One of these included the offer of a free LP in exchange for a financial gift, which was then to be directed to the artist of the donor's choice. The brochure represented a plea for individual Christians and church communities to be supportive of gospel artists. It reflected circumstances in which Christian performers found it hard to survive.

A commercial environment which left record companies and artists struggling to exist brought about an inevitable denouement. But economic realities only raise a prior question about the musical preferences of the evangelical community and why it was that performance based music did not attract greater popularity.

Entertainment Culture

The lack of support for Christian performance music is capable of a variety of interpretations. The success of praise and worship, which was usually music of an easy listening variety, suggests that performance music may have suffered because it was not normally of this type. As Christians continued to imitate the increasingly diverse sounds of the secular youth music scene, new styles did not have the broad appeal necessary to succeed in the Christian market. By the end of the 1970s, Christian bands were beginning to play music which reflected the punk style of groups like the Ramones and the Clash (Scott, 2003:83). Others like 100% Proof played a form of hard rock reminiscent of the secular band AC/DC (Scott, 2003:100). Such hard edged styles were far removed from the successful middle of the road format of praise and worship. Difficult music styles were not able to generate the support needed to survive within the limited evangelical marketplace.

It is also possible that Christian performance music declined because it was thought to be of poor quality. Malcolm Doney's description of Christian beat as 'mostly dreadful' may have been a view that was felt to be true of more recent evangelical music (cited in Scott, 2003:122). A correspondent to *Buzz* magazine in 1982, complained that Christian gospel artists were, 'Mere unheardof's, has beens, either too old or too out of date to make it in the secular scene' (*Buzz*, January 1982:9). Such Christians presumably preferred what they regarded as superior secular music to that of the evangelical sub-culture. Indeed, even those who did enjoy Christian music may not always have been entirely supportive. The members of After the Fire claimed that Christians recorded their work rather than purchase an album (Holloway, *Strait* 3, January 1982, Friends of After the Fire, 1999b) The same concern about illegal copying was reflected in Kingsway Music's brochure 'Something is seriously wrong with Christian music'. Another of its ideas for helping Christian artists was that consumers purchase 'Copyright Labels', which legitimised copying (Kingsway Music, 1981). Such unusual measures suggest that even those who did not regard Christian performance music as dreadful, were not so persuaded of its quality that they were always willing to pay for it. If Christian performance music struggled because of its challenging nature and because of a perception that it was second rate, it is also possible that it was harmed because of a sense of disillusion with its traditional outreach role.

Commending the Christian message was at the centre and core of the evangelical appropriation of modern music. From the outset it was seen as a vehicle to communicate faith. But as Christian performance music developed in the 1970s, it became clear that not every artist wanted to be identified with this kind of role. The debate around the basis upon which Christian performance music should operate was highlighted at the Greenbelt festival. Tony Jasper noted that by 1977 questions were already being asked about whether the gathering was about 'art' or 'ministry' (Jasper, 1984:138). By the early 1980s, he suggested that observers would notice an

> Ever widening gap between essentially 'ministry' and evangelistic bands and those 'which are made up of Christians but don't necessarily base their act around a particular Christian statement.'
>
> (Jasper, 1984:142)

This tension is easily observed. A high profile group like After the Fire, who did not speak about their faith from the stage felt obliged to explain their policy in Christian magazines (Tuffin, *Buzz*, December 1977, Friends of After the Fire, 199b, Holloway, *Strait 3*, January 1982, Friends of After the Fire, 1999b). The reluctance of bands to address audiences about matters of faith suggested to some evangelicals that the focus on evangelism had been lost; amid a preoccupation with celebrity and pop style adulation. Steve Goddard and Roger Green's interview with Larry Norman in which the artist, according to the interviewers, presented himself as an 'anti-hero' indicated his sensitivity to this issue. In spite of his rock star style, he presented himself as someone who didn't sign autographs, wasn't concerned with image and was just an 'ordinary' person (Goddard, Green, *Buzz*, May 1981, Official Larry Norman UK Website, 2004). Despite such protestations, personalities like Norman did not always appear as 'ordinary' and they were certainly not perceived as such. In *Buzz* magazine, an unhappy observer of the Greenbelt festival in 1981, noted the advance of celebrity culture in which Christian artists signed autographs in record tents (*Buzz*, November 1981:7). The following year, another letter suggested that Christian music 'was full of star dust and hype'. The trend was 'leading away from 'ministry and evangelism through music' and towards 'expensive Christian entertainment' (*Buzz*, January 1982:9). The perception that Christian folk, pop and rock music had betrayed its true purpose and had become a means of making celebrities and amusing

Christians was part of the story of performance music's failure to attract larger support. Indeed, a sense of disillusion with gospel artists seems to have provided the context for new thinking about the role of music and outreach.

In charismatic circles a view of evangelism which focused on worship, and especially the singing of modern worship songs was developed (Ward, 2005:205). The charismatic 'time of worship', a thirty or forty minute spot in which a number of songs were sung consecutively, came to be seen as a key place of encounter with God. Ward suggests that it became the equivalent of a sacrament, comparable to the place of the Mass for Catholics and the preached word for Protestants (Ward, 2005:199). The transformative power of worship was perceived not only to equip and mobilise Christians, but to be capable of influencing those who were outside the church. In his reflections upon his work with the charismatic praise group, Cloud, Philip Lawson-Johnston recounts how worship had become a 'powerful' evangelistic tool and that 'many' had been changed through the experience of worship (Lawson-Johnston, 1989:174). The Restoration churches were especially motivated by an Old Testament picture of 'the nations' won to the faith by the praises of God's people (Ward, 2005:135). The greatest expression of this kind of theology was the praise marches and the marches for Jesus which began in the late 1980s.

The praise marches were an initiative of the House and Restoration churches, but evangelicals from traditional churches were also involved (Ward, 2005:73, Walker, 1998:362-363). Thousands gathered on the streets of major cities to enact highly structured street liturgies, which included traditional elements as well as modern Christian songs (Walker, 1998:363). The theme of witness and Christian visibility was central, but there was also an idea that the marches could be seen as a kind of moral and spiritual disinfectant, changing behaviour by pronouncing defeat upon evil forces (Ward, 2005:73, Walker, 1998:364-365). The key point, is that all of this was perceived to be possible through worship, worship in which the praise and worship song had an important place. Outreach to the world had become intimately linked with congregational praise. It represented a very different strategy from the earlier attempts to communicate faith through Christian youth music in coffee bars and concert halls. The previous occasion when evangelicals had taken to the streets, at the Festival of Light in 1971 and 1972, they had done so with performance artists occupying an important role. Fifteen years or so later, that position was occupied by worshippers. The grounds of that change, whatever the theological justification, cannot be divorced from a sense of disillusionment with Christian performance music. Its failure to attract a wider audience among evangelicals involved a perception that it had become preoccupied with entertainment and notions of pop celebrity.

Despite the innovation and creativity which surrounded the emergence of Christian performance music it was not able to sustain itself in the United Kingdom. The failure to find a wider market for its music can be explained in a number of ways. The contentious nature of some musical styles and the perception that the music was of poor quality contributed to its decline. The sense that Christian performance music had lost its evangelistic focus also appears to have been a factor. Although Christian pop and rock music was a British invention, from the 1980s it was in the much larger evangelical community in the United States of America that it was ultimately to flourish.

Worship

At the end of the 1960s, there were hopes that more of the decade's musical revolution might be reflected in the worship of the church. In March 1969, the *Methodist Recorder* reported the deliberations of a youth conference held in Ashover, Derbyshire. The article was headed 'Worship 1969 style' and quoted from a statement released at its conclusion (*Methodist*

Recorder, 13 March 1969:18). In response to the question 'What style of worship do you want to see?' the conference communiqué declared:

> On the subject of music we felt that the organ had, in most instances, out stayed its usefulness and perhaps miniature orches-tra's could be substituted. The use of guitars seemed very popular. We felt choirs were out dated. Pop songs had a place in worship if they were relevant to the problems of today.
>
> (*Methodist Recorder*, 13 March 1969:18)

In the same year Peter D. Smith, the editor of the popular *Faith, Folk* series of song books expressed a similar optimism about new music within the church. At the height of folk music's popularity, in which it appeared to 'catch fire' within the church (Smith, *Methodist Recorder* 06 March 1969), he imagined a future in which the best elements of the past and present could be combined. Traditional material, which was 'still attractive and meaningful', could be blended with 'contemporary forms of expression in words, music, and movement' (Smith, *Methodist Recorder*, 01 May 1969).

In what follows, it will be seen that Smith's hopes for folk music were not realised, nor, apart from within evangelical and charismatic churches, was the band, guitar and pop mix of the Ashover youth. Following the pattern of the previous section, I will also attempt to suggest why optimism regarding musical change was ultimately unfulfilled. I begin with a consideration of folk music.

Folk Music

In chapter three it was noticed how the publication of church music supplements reflected the popularity of folk music during the latter half of the 1960s and the early 1970s. Music of this type continued to be sung over following years. Not least, because in an Anglican context the material from supplements was imported into new hymn books in a comprehensive manner.

In 1983 for example, the new edition of *Hymns Ancient and Modern, Hymns Ancient and Modern New Standard*, included all the material from two previous supplements (Rees, 1993:37). A similar process was to be observed in the *New English Hymnal* which contained three quarters of the previously published *English Praise* (*Church Times* review cited in Rees, 1993:41). In his review of *Hymns Ancient and Modern New Standard*, church musician Robin Rees expressed surprise that all of the previously published material 'passed muster' for inclusion in the new hymn book (Rees, 1993:37). It is difficult to avoid the conclusion that little thought was given to whether they were still the kind of songs that congregations wanted to sing. The compilers of the new Methodist hymn book, *Hymns and Psalms* (Methodist Church, 1983), appear to have been more thorough. The book attempted to be wide ranging in its choice of songs as was reflected by its full title; *Hymns and Psalms, A Methodist and Ecumenical Hymn Book* (Methodist Church, 1983:viii). It included songs of charismatic renewal, the work of new hymn writers, pop songs, traditional psalms and classical Methodist hymnody. Although it was represented, there was not a great deal of folk music. This is especially noticeable when it is compared with the experimental section of the earlier Methodist supplement. In 1969, half of the material in the songs section of *Hymns and Songs* was of the folk genre. In 1983, only three of those thirteen songs were seen as worthy of inclusion in the new book. Even more illuminating was the lack of material by Sydney Carter. There was no place for songs such as 'Lord of the Dance' and 'When I Needed a Neighbour'. 'One More Step' was the only Carter song included. Squeezed by other material, *Hymns and Psalms* clearly suggested that folk style no longer enjoyed its former popularity.

Hymns and Psalms did include new folk songs, such as 'Jesu, Jesu, Fill us with your Love', from the developing world (Methodist Publishing House, 1983:145). The process of locating and using folk styles from overseas has been continued by John Bell of the Iona Community. A minister in the Church of

Scotland, Bell was concerned with the task of renewing the churches worship in a direction which was not anchored in traditional hymnody or charismatic worship (Brink, 2006). His musical collaborations with Graham Maule and the Wild Goose Resource Group helped raise the profile of folk style within the church towards the end of the twentieth century. Yet, it remains the case that the latter half of the 1960s and the 1970s was the high point of the churches use of this style of music.

(1) Overexposure

One very practical cause of the waning fortunes of the popular folk music of the 1960s and 1970s may well have to do with overexposure. Sydney Carter's song 'Lord of the Dance' for example, became so well known that according to Nicholas Williams, who wrote the performers obituary in *The Independent*, it became part of the 'national psyche' (Williams, *The Independent*, 17 March 2004). In Ken Scott's collation of Christian albums from 1965 until 1985, he can say of a folk album that it contained 'the obligatory Sydney Carter song' (Scott: 2003:27). The difficulty with such well known, often repeated material is that eventually audiences grow weary. Such a fate may well have befallen a number of the popular folk songs from the 1960s. One likely candidate was Pete Seeger and Lee Hays' song 'If I had a hammer'. Although it was written in 1949, it became well known through its association with the American Civil Rights movement and its success in the pop charts. It was a hit for Peter, Paul and Mary in 1962 and Trini Lopez in 1963. Although a secular song of hope it was often used by Christians. It was included in *Faith, Folk and Clarity* and was one of two songs which came into the editor's mind when describing folk music's ability to express the hopes and needs of the world (Smith, *Methodist Recorder*, 01 May 1969:16). The song was used in worship, as can be seen from the earlier analysis of a special Christmas service held at Liverpool Cathedral in 1968. Its popularity among Christian young people and those connected to the church is evident through its frequent use at the MAYC London Weekend. It was part of the variety show for three consecutive years between 1964 and 1966 (*Methodist Recorder*, 04 June 1964:14, 03 June 1965:14, 19 June 1966:16). It would not be surprising if the repetition of 'If I had a hammer' and similar popular folk songs eventually lead to a cooling of enthusiasm for such pieces.

(2) The Turn Inwards

As was noticed in the earlier consideration of folk music, the genre's relevance for use in worship was located in its ability to affirm faith and to disturb it. Of these characteristics the latter was the most significant. It enabled Christians to demonstrate that their faith was relevant to all of life, including social and political issues. More pertinently, by singing songs such as 'If I had a hammer', they were able to associate themselves with the counter-culture ethos which looked for the world to be made a better place. However, as the 1960s gave way to the 1970s, cultural trends were moving against those who looked for outward manifestations of this through societal and political arrangements. The student protests of 1968 were the high point of those who were concerned with direct political action (Green, 1999:257). Those who were inspired by more general feelings of love and peace were disturbed by events which undermined confidence in the idea of an 'alternative society' in which these virtues could be expressed. A Rolling Stones concert at Altamont Speedway, California, in which the violence of Hells Angels brought about the death of an eighteen year old black man, was and is, commonly regarded as emblematic of the end of the utopian dreams of the counter-culture (Green, 1999:436). But there were other symbols, including the third Isle of Wight music festival, which highlighted rampant capitalist enterprise and communal divisions (Green, 1999:441). The end of the Beatles can also be included in this scenario of disillusion. As

Larry Norman pointed out: 'The Beatles said 'All you need is love' and then they broke up' (Norman, 1972:track 10). The effect of these events was to turn counter-cultural sentiment away from the transformation of the world through communal co-operation and towards one of its other concerns, namely the transformation of the individual (Green, 1999:245-247). Mention has already been made of how the impact of this was experienced within the world of folk music. According to Michael Brocken, it became less concerned with overt politicising and 'more with agency for cultural change on a personal level' (Brocken, 2003:111). The alteration of the cultural zeitgeist seems to have been mirrored in the church. Evangelical folk music which majored on the possibility of personal transformation grew in popularity. On the other hand, the kind of folk music which was linked with counter-cultural hopes of a better world now looked dated. As utopian aspirations faded away, so did the church music which had been most associated with it.

(3) Hymn Competition

The Christian use of folk protest songs in its worship and work allowed it to be associated with the counter-cultural aspirations of the 1960s. However, there was also a very practical reason why it used this material. This was because the age of its hymnals prevented Christians from satisfactorily engaging with contemporary issues. In the Church of England, the *English Hymnal* was first published in 1906 and had only minor revision in 1933 (Rees, 1993:37-38). Its main rival within the Anglican community, *Hymns Ancient and Modern* was revised in 1950 but was essentially a 'pre-war book' (Luff, *New Christian*, 13 December 1969:12). The Methodist Church was using a hymn book which had remained unchanged since its publication in 1932. There was little in such volumes that related directly to the challenges of the 1960s. When within weeks of each other in 1969, supplements were published for *Hymns*

Ancient and Modern and the *Methodist Hymn Book,* the music critic of the *New Christian,* Alan Luff, posed what he considered was the key question: 'Are we to be able to sing about the things we need to sing about – World Peace and Hunger, Christian Unity, Industry, Service of Others, Race Relations?' (Luff, *New Christian,* 13 November 1969:12). The answer Luff gave was affirming, even though he considered that there was not enough material reflecting contemporary issues. The key point, however, is that the songs that were included of this type were not just of a folk style.

The new supplements reflected the growth in new hymn writing that had been talking place during the 1960s and was associated with names such as G. W. Briggs, Timothy Rees, Fred Kaan, D.W. Hughes and F. Pratt Green. In contrast to some of the folk material, the songs were written from a distinctly Christian point of view. The Anglican supplement, *100 Hundred Hymns for Today* for example, included Kaan's hymn 'For the Healing of the Nations':

> For the healing of the nations,
> Lord, we pray with one accord,
> for a just and equal sharing
> of the things that earth affords.
> To a life of love in action
> help us rise and pledge our word.
>
> Lead us forward into freedom,
> from despair your world release,
> that, redeemed from war and hatred,
> all may come and go in peace.
> Show us how through care and goodness
> fear will die and hope increase.
>
> All that kills abundant living,
> let it from the earth be banned:
> pride of status, race or schooling,

dogmas that obscure your plan.
In our common quest for justice
may we hallow brief life's span.

You, Creator God, have written
your great name on humankind;
for our growing in your likeness
bring the life of Christ to mind;
that by our response and service
earth its destiny may find.

(Kaan, 1969:28)

As the first supplements were joined by others in the 1970s and then in the 1980s by new hymn books, the numbers of this type of song increased. It meant that Christians who wanted to express a social and political concern could do so without recourse to folk music. Moreover, it meant that they could so from an overtly Christian perspective. The growth of a contemporary hymnody which was able to grapple with contemporary issues from a Christian point of view appears to have contributed to the decline of folk music within the church.

Following its popularity in the late 1960s and early 1970s, a number of factors appear to have adversely affected the fortunes of folk music within the church. As a consequence of its success it was over exposed, it was the victim of a changing cultural climate and its monopoly as a means of expressing concern about issues of justice and peace was lost. The case of the other style of 1960s worship music which was grounded in folk must now be considered. From the simple folk songs of the early charismatic renewal, the genre of praise and worship increasingly appropriated a pop sensitivity and became increasingly popular within the evangelical and charismatic sections of the church during the 1980s. Yet, as the following will show, its largely mellow sound did not allow it to extend its appeal significantly beyond its own constituency.

Praise and Worship

The songs of charismatic renewal touched the life of traditional congregations through a variety of means. One of these was the publication of song books which included old and new material. The Methodist book *Hymns and Psalms* reflected this strategy on a small scale, but perhaps the most significant was *Mission Praise* (Mission England Praise, 1983). First published in connection with a series of large scale evangelistic events involving Billy Graham, entitled 'Mission England' in 1984, it exposed the genre of praise and worship to a wide audience. In the Church of England for example, this can be seen in The Report of the Archbishops' Commission on Church Music, *In Tune with Heaven,* which was published in 1992. The report included a musical survey designed to indicate the state of church music across the denomination (Archbishops', 1992:77). It discovered that thirty six per cent of sampled churches used *Mission Praise* or the related publication *Junior Praise*. It was the 'most popular' song book and although mainly used by evangelical or charismatic churches, it was also used by seventeen per cent of churches outside this part of the church (Archbishops', 1992:275). Because of the variety of song books available to Anglican churches this did not mean that it was the most used or the basic hymn book of those questioned (Rees, 1993:150-151). But it does indicate how congregations outside the evangelical and charismatic constituency were exposed to songs of praise and worship. The ease with which new songs could be reproduced by photocopying and overhead projectors may have aided the crossover of charismatic songs into the wider church. Although these devices were frequently used by evangelicals and charismatics, they also seem to have been used by those of a different spiritual outlook (Rees, 1993:151, Ward, 2005:82-83). It is also possible that a recognition of the quality of some of Graham Kendrick's songs contributed to the spread of new, charismatic material (Wilson-Dickson, 1992:416).

Although praise and worship songs managed to transcend their origin in the charismatic movement, once out of that environment they were unlikely to be accompanied by instruments reflecting a folk pop style. Music or worship groups were much less likely to be found in churches outside evangelical and charismatic circles. The *Music in Parish Worship* statistical survey of 1986 for example, revealed that where as forty four per cent of Anglican evangelical churches had a music group, this was only true of thirteen per cent of central and thirteen per cent of catholic parts of the church (cited in Sinclair, 1992:12). Indeed, the limited nature of the wider churches appropriation of the praise and worship genre is best illustrated by the persistence of traditional forms of musical accompaniment.

The Report of the Archbishops' Commission on Church Music found that 'organ music retains its popularity' (Archbishops', 1992:79). It reported that eighty five per cent of churches continued to use the instrument in its repertoire of music, nearly two thirds had a choir and that psalms sung to Anglican chant was still to be heard in seventy four per cent of churches (Archbishops', 1992:77-79). The research of Rees in 1993, confirmed the prevalence of traditional forms, a typical service would 'almost certainly' involve accompaniment by an organ and there would be a 50/50 chance of a choir (Rees, 1993:165). Within the Methodist Church, a survey of its minister's revealed that a significant number favoured alternatives to the church organ. John M. Haley and Leslie J. Francis contacted seventy four per cent of Methodist clergy and in a wide ranging piece of research, they found that sixty eight per cent agreed with the statement 'that Methodist worship depends too much on the organ' (Haley and Francis, 2006:85). That so many clergy approved of this assertion strongly suggested that Methodist worship was dominated by musical accompaniment of a traditional kind. Although praise and worship style penetrated the worshipping life of traditional churches it was ultimately unable to reach out beyond the evangelical and charismatic constituency.

By the 1980s, charismatic praise had been a feature of the ecclesial landscape long enough to enable critics and supporters to engage. This was most noticeable in the essays edited by Robin Sheldon under the title *In Spirit and in Truth*. In another collection of articles, David Martin and Peter Mullen's *Strange Gifts?* considered the charismatic movement as a whole, but also contained material with a music focus. An examination of some of these essays offers insights into why the mild, folk pop fusion of praise and worship did not win acceptance across the churches.

(1) Inferior

One of the most polemical of the essays to be found in *Strange Gifts?* was that by one of the editors, the Reverend Peter Mullen. Mullen was a writer and a broadcaster and was already known for his caustic criticisms of charismatic renewal. Earlier in 1984 for example, the *Guardian* newspaper had published one of his most critical articles, which was entitled 'The curse of the hallelujah chorus' (*Guardian*, 28 July 1984) His article in *Strange Gifts?* continued in this vein. As far as charismatic praise was concerned he condemned it by associating it with inferior pop culture. In a comparison with current television shows he suggested that it was not to be compared with lower quality religious programming, but was closer to more dubious popular entertainment. 'This is not liturgy – the theatre of the soul' he argued, 'It is not even *Stars on Sunday*; it is *Game for a Laugh* transposed to the sanctuary' (Mullen, 1984:103). *Game for a Laugh* was a television series which revolved around the performance of practical jokes upon unsuspecting individuals, which some critics considered to be in poor taste (Game for a Laugh, 2001). By linking this with praise and worship, Mullen suggested that charismatic music represented the worst kind of pop culture. He considered it to be 'unimaginative guitar music' and 'stuff that sounds like failed Andrew Lloyd Webber' (Mullen, 1984:103). Mullen's polemic indicated the strength of feeling that was generated by the subject. This is reflected by the essay of Philip Lawson-Smith, who was part of the charismatic worship scene. When he represented the comments of those who were not favourably disposed towards the kind of music he performed, he used such words as 'noise', 'irreverent', 'brash' and 'loud' and he was aware that to those with musical training it was 'unbearable' (Lawson-Johnston, 1989:161-162). From their different perspectives, Mullen and Lawson-Johnston grant us a sense of the concern that existed about the musical quality of worship songs. The perception of inferiority was a factor in the failure of charismatic praise to win the approval of traditional worshippers.

(2) Emotional

Charismatic worship introduced phenomena that were not common to traditional Protestant worship. These included speaking in tongues, dance, the raising of hands and shouts of acclamation. They were often accompanied with 'great emotional investment' which was not to everyone's taste (Davis, 1984:121). In his contribution to *Strange Gifts?*, the Reverend Ronald Noakes, a former medical missionary to sea men and forces chaplain, considered the 'strongly emotional content' of charismatic worship to be a form of 'herd instinct' (Noakes, 1984:159ff). Noakes' views were based on the work of the Frenchman, Gustave Le Bon, who attributed, what he considered was the absence of the rational element in religion, to 'crowd psychology'. Noakes explained:

> Everyone who forms part of a crowd to hear a speaker is actually acted upon by a form of herd suggestion, and this comes about by the impact of all who are being influenced by the orator. By singing or by shouting or merely by clapping, a crowd is often worked up into an emotional and almost hypnotic state into which suggestions are easily implanted. If, on such occasions, there is affirmation – such as shouts of 'Here, here', 'Hallelujah' or 'Go on, Sir' –

then suggestion is heightened considerably and beliefs may be changed.

(Noakes, 1984:160)

Noakes considered that the campaigns of Billy Graham were examples of herd instinct and that it was clearly manifested in the charismatic movement. In this regard, the role of music was thought to be important. Noakes argued:

> The worship of the charismatic movement has a great number of hymns, each with a strong emotional content. Choruses are repeated again and again until the congregation is in a slightly emotional state. Sometimes this state clearly resembles attacks of hysteria.

(Noakes, 1984:161)

While Noakes' scholarly explanation of charismatic worship was unusual, it did reflect a general concern about its emotional nature. Lawson-Johnston's account of critical observations included comments about the repetitive nature of praise songs and that the worship of which they were a part was 'over emotional' (Lawson-Johnston, 1989:161-162). Similarly, Mullen criticised the combination of what he considered to be 'frivolous enthusiasm' with repetitive guitar playing (Mullen, 1984:103). The emotion that was associated with charismatic worship songs did not appeal to those who desired a more reasonable religion. Noakes considered that the remedy for charismatic emotionalism was a 'proper respect for the traditional values' of the Anglican church (Noakes, 1984:161).

(3) Escapist

The claim that charismatic worship was escapist was made by Graham Cray in the collection of essays edited by Robin Sheldon. The fact that at the time of writing the author was leading a thriving charismatic congregation in York, and a supporter of

175

the Holy Spirit renewal movement, made his comment particularly significant (Cray, 1989:1, 11). Cray's contribution to *In Spirit and in Truth* argued that charismatic spirituality had so emphasised the themes of Jesus Lordship and triumph that it had produced an 'other worldly religion', neglectful of the real world of suffering and pain. This had been reflected in the melodies and the rhythms of praise and worship songs (Cray, 1989:12). Cray was particularly keen to stress the need for his tradition to develop a spirituality which took seriously the pain of social injustice (Cray, 1989:4ff). Such an alteration would involve musical changes:

> There will need to be a renewal of musical content and form. We shall need to find a form which is a suitable vehicle to express longing, suffering, and hope as well as triumph, faith and doctrinal certainty.

> (Cray, 1989:14)

The escapism to which Cray drew attention, also featured in Mullen's critique of the charismatic movement. In his article 'Confusion Worse Confounded', he was particularly concerned with its stress on supernatural healing and the idea of some, that it was 'always' God's will to heal. He considered it a failure to properly engage with the everyday realities of disease, cancer and coronary thrombosis (Mullen, 1984:101). Mullen didn't make any direct musical link, although it may have been in mind when he made reference to the shallow spirituality of the worship song (Mullen, 1984:103). An explicit link was made by John Bell of the Iona Community, who in a similar fashion to Cray, argued that by focussing on the majesty and exaltation of God, worship songs had ignored 'expressions of anger, doubt, bewilderment and sorrow' (Bell, 2003:110). For those who were directly affected by such issues and for those who wanted to sing about matters of justice and peace the worship song was seldom of use. A stress on divine power and victory and a consequent failure to engage with the entirety of the human condition, may also have contributed to its lack of appeal in certain parts of the church.

The praise and worship song of the charismatic renewal was the most popular appropriation of 1960s youth musical styles. In the middle of the 1990s, it was refashioned to reflect a rock style, although this was by no means universally adopted (Powell, 2003:672). Yet, even in its milder form it was not able to extend its appeal much beyond that of evangelical and charismatic churches. Concerns about its musical style and its association with what were perceived as unpalatable aspects of charismatic spirituality appear to have been the sources of this.

Looking Back

This chapter has shown that the momentum which was gained through an initial, wide ranging engagement with the youth music of the 1960s was not sustained by the Christian churches. At the end of the millennium, traditional styles still dominated ecclesial worship and Christian performance music declined rapidly from the relatively high profile it acquired during the 1970s and the early 1980s. Of course, more modern styles were not absent towards the latter part of the twentieth century. Praise and worship flourished within its own evangelical constituency and as we have noted, examples of Christian engagement with folk, pop and rock music persisted. Yet overall, the picture was not one which might have suggested that there had been a musical revolution a few decades earlier. There were, as I have suggested, a number of reasons for this state of affairs. Not all of them were directly related to a dislike of contemporary music. Cultural trends, such as the fragmentation of the youth music scene and the demise of the counter-culture, changes within the church, such as the growth of modern hymnody, and negative associations, such as praise and worship's link with charismatic spirituality, all played a role in sapping enthusiasm for modern sounds. In combination with attitudes which did express an aversion to youth music styles the effect was corrosive. It can only be represented as a decline compared to the enthusiastic way in which Christians had earlier engaged with the youth music of the 1960s.

Opposition to 1960s youth music, and especially its use in the church, was expressed with vigour by Christian critics. But contrary to the views of social historians like Martin, Segrave, Cloonan and Street, they did not represent the only attitude within the church. This study has observed an extraordinary burst of Christian creativity, ranging from simple folk songs to complex progressive rock. It is almost too obvious to say, in contrast to Sandbrook, that this was not just the work of Christian leaders. Clergy played important roles, especially during the beat and folk eras, but essentially the Christian appropriation of 1960s youth music was a lay movement, involving individuals with only rudimentary skills to those who were trained musicians. They were the first Christians to engage with electric music and laid the foundation for all future interaction with contemporary styles. The new music was used in a variety of ways. It was put into service as a tool of outreach, as a way of expressing concern about the world and it was used in worship. Behind all this creativity, lay the thought that youth styles were suitable forms of music for Christians to appropriate. The Devil was not to have all the good music.

7

Soundings

The controversy which first marked Christian's use of contemporary musical styles in the 1960s has not dissipated with time. In today's church the strength of feeling surrounding the issue of music in worship is as strong as ever.

I attended a service of welcome and induction of a new priest. The church had previously been led by a charismatic clergyman and the singing was accompanied by an organ and by a music group. At the welcome, I was invited to sit near the bishop's wife. Glancing at the order of service, I noted that the first hymn was 'Love divine' by Charles Wesley. The bishop's wife replied with some conviction that it would be the only worth while musical item that we would be singing. She had taken time to observe that all the other pieces were of a rather more recent vintage than that by Mr Wesley. At the end of the service, without any prompting on my part, she affirmed that her initial analysis of the musical content had been correct. In a Methodist context, something of the heat generated by the subject of church music can be seen by the correspondence which took place in the *Methodist Recorder* during the latter part of 2004 and early 2005. Prompted by an article by Tony Jasper in which he complained about the serviceability of *Hymn and Psalms*, (the largely traditional Methodist hymn book), for contemporary use, it provoked a wide ranging discussion and diverse views. For example, a J.V. Bassill spoke highly of the hymn book: 'There is so much to explore here compared to the very thin content of the words of so many newer songs' (Bassill, *Methodist Recorder*, 09.12.04). Taking a different view, a John Foster, implied that if churches wished to flourish they should use modern styles, 'the fastest growing churches have abandoned (or all but) hymn music altogether', he argued (Foster, *Methodist Recorder*, 20.01.05). With such different perspectives, it is perhaps not surprising that the researchers John M. Haley and Leslie J. Francis, report anecdotal evidence of 'worship wars' in some Methodist church's (Haley and Francis, 2006:82). There is every reason to think that the nature of music to be used in worship has continued to be a source of conflict in other denominations also.

In this final chapter, it is the contemporary context that I wish to briefly address. The focus will be upon music in church worship, rather than performance music, as this is the most contentious area, where everyone, it seems, has an opinion. By looking back at the story that has been told over the previous pages, the aim is to draw out a number of salient themes which are still pertinent for any consideration of music and worship today. It will quickly be perceived, that I believe the story of Christian engagement with 1960s youth music poses the greatest challenge to the wider church, rather than to evangelicals and charismatics. Perhaps I should say at the outset then, that I do not consider myself a musical revolutionary. Most of my adult life I have worked in churches which have normally used traditional forms of accompaniment. I am aware of the difficulties that some Christians have with this issue. I have no great desire to banish the treasures of our musical heritage. But I do believe that the modern church needs to acquire a sense of musical adventure and courage that was typical of the 1960s pioneers.

Association

This study has shown how music is a source of powerful associations. These linkages had important implications for their Christian use in the 1960s and 1970s. Folk music for example, was overflowing with positive associations, which made it a suitable vehicle for Christian appropriation. However, pop and rock were subject to rather different emotions. The links with sexual immorality, commercialism and harmful behaviours made it, (from some Christian perspectives), an implausible candidate for use. The same kinds of sentiments were felt by those outside the church. As we saw in the introduction, the social historian, John Street, found the concerns of rock music incompatible with religious worship. The Christian rock band, After the Fire, came across the same attitude among rock journalists. Within and without the church, the unholy associations of pop and rock music determined that such music was unfit for purpose. It was not a novel response. Some of the greatest composers of traditional church music were also employed in creating works for a secular market; they often used similar musical styles for both environments (Wilson-Dickson, 1992:118-119, 209ff). Andrew Wilson-Dickson, for example, draws attention to J.S. Bach's willingness to appropriate 'the fashionable musical styles of the day' and how this was not well received by some Christians when applied to a church context:

When in a large town (Bach's) Passion Music was done for the first time, with twelve violins, many oboes, bassoons, and other instruments, many people were astounded and did not know what to make of it. In the pew of a noble family in church, many Ministers and Noble ladies were present, who sang the first Passion chorale out of their books with great devotion. But when this theatrical music began, all these people were thrown into the greatest bewilderment, looked at each other and said: 'What will come of this?' An old widow of the nobility said: 'God save us, my children! It's just as if we were at an Opera Comedy.' But everyone was genuinely displeased by it and voiced just complaints against it.

(cited in Wilson-Dickson, 1992:157)

A concern about the worldly associations of certain types of music has a long history, for some Christians it has meant that they were deemed unfit for divine service.

The mention of early reactions to the work of Bach is a reminder that, powerful as musical associations can be, they are not unchangeable. Few would connect Bach with impious theatrical music today. In recent times, one can notice a change in the affinities that surround pop and rock music. For example, no longer are they associated with youth in quite the same way as they were in the 1960s and 1970s. Not only do ageing stars from that era continue to perform successfully, but their contemporaries have continued to enjoy pop and rock styles. The associations that readily attach themselves to music are not an iron grid which rigidly determines how music is to be interpreted. Through a multiple of factors they change with time and indeed, can be challenged. It is this which I consider to be one of the greatest achievements of the Christian pop and rock artists of the 1960s and 1970s. They were prepared to confront conventions which suggested that Christianity and pop and rock music were unlikely partners. This meant not only enjoying youth music for pleasure but also appropriating it in the service of the gospel.

The work of young Christian artists in the 1960s and 1970s illustrates that powerful musical associations can be questioned and defied. I believe it to have an important contemporary challenge for the worshipping life of the church, especially to that part of the church which is not evangelical or charismatic. For it is my view, that the modern church is increasingly bound by a musical convention. It is a rule which associates contemporary musical styles with the theologically conservative side of the church. In the last chapter, I suggested that the wider church was unwilling to appropriate worship songs because of their association with charismatic spirituality. The outcome is that the connection between charismatics, evangelicals and modern expressions has become so strong as to be coterminous. Indeed, their interpretation of contemporary worshipping style has become the interpretation. The wider church appears to have evacuated the field of musical relevance for fear of being associated with theological conservatism. Much as one might understand such an attitude, one wonders about its wisdom. It might have, and could still pursue, a rather different policy. Instead of avoidance, it could attempt to do what we have seen was done in the 1960s and 1970s. Namely, challenge musical associations. In this case, the link that is evident between contemporary expressions and charismatic spirituality. If Christians could challenge the idea that faith and youth music were incompatible, cannot the wider church challenge the notion that modern Christian music must always mean the charismatic worship song? The folk idiom, currently resurgent could be exploited. Other musical genres might be used. The pop folk fusion itself could be refashioned in a way which could be acceptable to the wider church. Indeed, some of the better worship songs have a lyrical and theological content which have made them widely acceptable. Nor is the music inevitably as poor, as some critics have tried to suggest. The genre could be exploited in a way which would have greater appeal to those who do not see themselves as charismatic or evangelical. The issue is whether anyone will rise to the challenge. There are those who might ask about the purpose of such a proposal. The story of 1960s engagement with youth music offers at least one important suggestion.

Intelligibility

The use of secular styles of music in church worship was frequently motivated by the need to provide a sound that made sense to young people. In the second half of the twentieth century it was a tradition that began with Father Geoffrey Beaumont's revision of the mass and is noticeable in the development of beat services and the use of folk. The success of praise and worship owed much to an inclusive musical formula, which allowed some sort of connection to be made between modern sounds and worship. Beaumont stressed new music's ability to make people feel 'comfortable' in a church context, Edward H. Patey considered that it eased communication and Peter D. Smith focussed on folk's ability to convey relevance. In contrast to traditional church music, which was considered to be impenetrable to young people, modern styles enabled the church to relate its faith in an intelligible way. It helped remove, what might be described, as some of the 'strangeness' of Christian worship.

To many under fifty, let alone those who are teenagers, much of traditional church music remains an alien sound. The Reverend Brian Bird's comment, made in 1958, that traditional church music was 'utterly incomprehensible' to the average person remains an extraordinarily apt comment fifty years later. In an age when contemporary styles of music provide the backdrop against which so many live their lives, to be so seriously out of step, as the church frequently is, can only reduce its pastoral and missionary effectiveness. There is an obvious need for a serious consideration of how the church might reflect contemporary musical styles and present itself and its message in a relevant way.

One of the great ironies regarding the issue of church music and intelligibility is that in other areas it has made enormous efforts to ensure that it can connect with modernity. A very obvious example is that of language. The words that are used in most church services today are remarkably different from what was typical sixty years ago. In the 1950s there were few modern translations of the bible. The liturgy and most of the hymnody reflected a dead language in which congregations were invited to speak of 'ye', 'thee' and 'thou'. The second half of the twentieth century witnessed a huge effort to transform this situation. Modern translations of the bible and new service books became common. As we saw, hymn book supplements and then new hymn books, gave a significant place to new hymn writers who not only addressed topical issues, but used everyday English. Inevitably, such changes were not to everyone's liking, but the reforms have been widely appropriated. The purpose of this activity was clear. It concerned the need for worship to be intelligible, both for those who attended regularly and for those who stood on the periphery. Christians altered their speech in order to relate to modern realities. The implications of this for music, however, do not seem to have been widely appreciated. But it is difficult to avoid them. If the intelligibility of language in worship has been important enough to revise bibles, service books and hymns, (at enormous financial cost), it is difficult to see why it should not also apply to musical styles.

The irony that a church concerned with vernacular expressions should fail to apply this to music is matched by one other. Evangelicals and charismatics who have been committed to the idea of the musical vernacular have not been so dedicated to the principle when it concerns words. As was noted, ancient biblical images and the language of old English is a common feature of their songs. Instead of attempting the (admittedly) difficult task of using contemporary words and images, songs include references to verbs such as 'exalt', 'magnify', 'extol' and 'anoint' and nouns such as 'fortress', 'banner' 'throne' and 'Zion' (Page, 2004:90ff). Nick Page's analysis of a thousand modern songs revealed only fourteen distinctively modern images. He summarised:

> You can find flocks of lambs, vats of anointing oil, enough two edged swords and chariots to stock an army. But no cars. No electricity. No Internet, newspapers or TV.
>
> (Page, 2004:99)

The effect is that some songs are as difficult to understand as the ancient hymns they were designed to replace. Contemporary sounds still need intelligible lyrics if they are to be of service to the church, the gospel and the God we serve.

There is a great need in the church today to use the vernacular in both music and lyrics. It can be done and the better worship songs have achieved this. Some of the songs of Graham Kendrick for example, illustrate what is possible. But to be equally serious about words and sounds presents a challenge to all. Evangelicals need to appreciate that scripture songs are not always enough. Intelligibility requires that biblical themes are allowed to live through the use of modern words and imagery. Traditionalists, on the other hand, need to appreciate that it is not just words that matter.

Diversity

The 1960s was a period of intense musical creativity within the churches of the United Kingdom. An extraordinary variety of pop, folk, rock and various fusions of these were produced. In evangelistic coffee bars, in concerts and in Christian celebrations of the arts (like Greenbelt for example), these diverse styles mingled. The range was never so extensive within the context of church worship. But even here, there were attempts to combine traditional church music with pop, folk and the folk pop fusion of the worship song. It was a phenomenon that deserves to be explored again today. The requirements of congregational participation do inevitably constrain what might be considered appropriate for use. But in a world which has seen an explosion of musical genres, (continuing the trend of the musical fusion of the 1960s), the very limited range that churches provide can only be described as inadequate. In a multicoloured musical culture, the churches frequently offer just one or two musical colours. Of course, it could be argued that a range of musical genres ultimately pleases no one. Such has been part of the rationale for some forms of fresh expressions and alternative worship. I do not deny that responding to specific groups may need a particular musical expression. However, the increasingly diverse musical context in which we live has, I believe, extended the breadth of taste. In some unscientific explorations of my own, I discovered that Christian people under the age of fifty five years seldom described their musical taste as limited to one genre. Given a choice of ten types of music (from classical to rock), plus an 'other' option, only nine per cent expressed a solitary preference. There is a musical openness today, which perhaps, was not true of the recent past. A person can, as happened to me recently, talk of the possibility of exploring opera, while at the same time look forward to seeing the next tour by the pop rock band Keane. Such a scenario makes an exploration of musical diversity within the church a genuine possibility.

The quest for diverse sounds will inevitably be difficult for those who treasure the sound of organ and choir. As I said at the beginning of this chapter, I have no desire to see that tradition terminated, but the monopoly that it enjoys in many places, needs to give way to a musical pluralism. Not least, ironically, because although musical tastes are expanding, they seem not to be doing so in a way which embraces the music traditionally associated with the church. In my own research for example, while a sizeable number of Christians under fifty five years of age continued to enjoy classical music, (nearly half), support for choral music was at only eighteen per cent. For those under thirty years of age it was down to fifteen per cent. One suspects, (although I have no figures for this), that the support of organ music for those less than fifty five years of age is probably as poor, if not worse. If the purpose of life, including public worship, is, as the Psalms, Augustine and Calvin suggest, to glorify God and enjoy him for ever, then there is a need to embrace musical genres which encourage that possibility. It suggests a less prominent role for traditional styles.

Beyond the tastes of modern people, there is of course, a rather more theological reason for embracing musical diversity in the church. If music in all its variety is God's gift, it is difficult to see why only certain varieties should be used by the church. At the end of Jane Sinclair's response to the Archbishops' *In Tune with Heaven* report, there is a cartoon. It depicts a clergyman eulogising God's gift of music. The figure extols a great long list of musical genres. 'The list is endless' he exclaims,

'what a gift indeed'. In the final picture we are shown the clergyman announcing the next hymn, 'The Lords my Shepherd' to
the tune 'Crimond' (Sinclair, 1992:25). It is an accurate presentation of how the church says one thing and does another. The
diverse Christian music of the 1960s should encourage churches
to consider whether they are doing justice to God's great gift of
music.

The musical experience of the parts of the 1960s church,
which involved engagement, courage, creativity and the use of
new styles, has then, some challenging things to say to the
modern church. I have no illusions about the way some of my
suggestions will be heard. Or, if deemed at all appropriate, the
difficulty of applying them. I am equally sure, unless the church
is happy to remain a cultural backwater, removed and apart
from all semblance of contemporary life, it needs to change.

Bibliography

Adorno, T.W. (1990) 'On Popular Music' in S. Frith and A. Goodwin (eds), *On Record: Rock, Pop, and the Written Word*, Routledge.

Alfonso, B. (2002) *The Billboard Guide to Contemporary Christian Music*, Billboard Books.

Ainger, G. (1969) 'Christ in Need' in Methodist Church, *Hymns and Songs*, Methodist Publishing House.

Appleford, S. (1997) *The Rolling Stones, It's Only Rock and Roll: Song by Song*, Schirmer Books.

Anderson, I. (2003) 'Folk Rock' in P.D. Noyer (ed.), *The Illustrated Encyclopedia of Music*, Flame Tree Publishing.

Archbishops' Commission on Church Music (1992) *In Tune with Heaven*, London: Church House Publishing.

Bebbington, D.W. (1989) *Evangelicalism in Modern Britain: A History from the 1730s to the 1980s*, London: Unwin Hyman Ltd.

Bell, J. (2003) 'The Lost Tradition of Lament' in S. Darlington and A. Kreider (eds), *Composing Music for Worship*, Canterbury Press, Norwich.

Bernstein, G.L. (2004) *The Myth of Decline: The Rise of Britain since 1945*, Pimlico.

Bird, B. (1958) *Skiffle*, Robert Hale Ltd.

Black, J. (2004) 'A Tale of Two Cities' in P. Trynka (ed.), *The Beatles: Ten Years that Shook the World*, Dorling Kindersley Ltd.

Boons, B. (2005) *Rhythm Finds its Groove* [internet]. Available from: <http://www.joystrings.co.uk/Rhythm_finds_its_Groove.pdf > [Accessed 06 July 2005].

Boyes, E. and Knowles, E. (1965) *Crazy Mixed up Generation* [internet] Available from: <http://www.liv.ac.uk-u04/crossbeats/songs.htm> [Accessed 08 July 2005].

Boyes, G. (1993) *The Imagined Village: Culture, Ideology and the English Folk Revival*, Manchester University Press.

Brierley, P. (2000) *The Tide is Running Out*, London: Christian Research.

Brown, F.B. (2000) *Good Taste, Bad Taste and Christian Taste: Aesthetics in Religious Life*, Oxford University Press.

Buskin, R. (2003) 'Psychedelic Rock, Rock 'n' Roll' in P.D. Noyer (ed.), *The Illustrated Encyclopedia of Music*, Flame Tree Publishing.

Bradley, D. (1992) *Understanding Rock 'n' Roll: Popular Music in Britain 1955-1964*, Oxford, Oxford University Press.

Brink, E.R. (2006) *For whom the Bell Toils: An Interview with John bell of the Iona Community* [internet]. Available from: <http://reformed- worship.org/magazine/article.cfm ?article_id=637> [Accessed 24 May 2007].

Brocken, M. (2003) *The British Folk Revival*, Ashgate Publishing Ltd.

Brown, C.G. (2001) *The Death of Christian Britain*, Routledge.

Carr, J. (1999) *Dancing in the Shadows: The Story of After the Fire* [internet]. Available from: <http://friends.afterthefire.co.uk/atfhistory.htm> [Accessed 09 May 2007].

Carter, S. (1967) 'Son of Man' in P. D. Smith (ed.), *Faith, Folk and Clarity*, Galliard Ltd.

Chambers, I. (1985) *Urban Rhythms*, Macmillan Education Ltd.

Christian Aid (1970) *Songs from the Square*, Brian Frost.

Cleall, C. (1964) *Music and Holiness*, Epworth Press.

Clements, K.W. (1988) *Lovers of Discord: Twentieth Theological Controversies in England*, SPCK.

Cloonan, M. (1996) *Banned! Censorship of Popular Music in Britain: 1967-92*, Arena, Ashgate Publishing.

Cobb, K. (2005) *The Blackwell Guide to Theology and Popular Culture*, Blackwell Publishing Ltd.

Cray, G. (1989) 'Justice, Rock and the Renewal of Worship' in R. Sheldon (Ed.), *In Spirit and in Truth*, Hodder & Stoughton.

Crossbeats (2004a) *Crossbeats Bookings* [internet]. Available from: <http://www.liv.ac. uk-qu04/crossbeats/bookinglist.htm> [Accessed 23 March 2007].

Crossbeats (2004b) *Crossbeats Members* [internet]. Available from: <http://www.liv.ac. uk-qu04/www.crossbeats/members> [Accessed 16 June 2005].

Crossbeats (2004c) *The Changing Contemporary Christian Music Scene* [internet]. Available from: <http://liv.ac.uk-qu04/www.crossbeats/growthccm.htm> [Accessed 05 July 2005].

Crossbeats (2004d) *The Explosion (and Decay?) of Coffee Bar Evangelism* [internet]. Available from: <http://liv.ac.uk-qu04/www.crossbeats/ coffee.htm> [Accessed 28 March 2007].

Crossbeats (2004e) *Words of Songs by the Crossbeats* [internet]. Available from: <http://www.liv.ac.uk-qu04/crossbeats/songs.htm> [Accessed 08 July 2005].

Crossbeats (2004f) *John Banner Manager of the Crossbeats* [internet]. Available from: <http://www.liv.ac.uk-qu04/crossbeats/y65jwb.htm> [Accessed 05 July 2005].

Crossbeats (2004g) *Buzz Magazine* [internet]. Available from: <http://www.liv.ac.uk-qu04/crossbeats/buzz.htm> [Accessed 12 July 2005].

Crossbeats (2004h) *Prayer Partners* [internet]. Available from: <http://www.liv.ac.uk-qu04/crossbeats/prayer.htm> [Accessed 05 July 2005].

Crossbeats (2004i) *Music at St Leonard's* [internet]. Available from: <http://www.liv. ac.uk-qu04/crossbeats/y62ysing.htm> [Accessed 05 July 2005].

Crossbeats (2004j) *Cheadle Parish Church* [internet]. Available from: <http://www.liv. ac.uk-qu04/crossbeats/cheadlepc.htm> [Accessed 28 March 2007].

Crossbeats (2004k) *First Singles' Release* [internet]. Available from: <http://www.liv. ac.uk-qu04/crossbeats/y66sngfly.htm> [Accessed 23 March 2007].

Dakers, L. (1989) 'The Establishment and the Need for Change' in R. Sheldon (ed.), *In Spirit in Truth*, Hodder & Stoughton.

Dakers, L. (1995) *Places where they Sing*, Canterbury Press, Norwich.

Darden, R. (2004) *People get Ready: A New History of Black Gospel Music*, The Continuum International Publishing Group Inc.

Davis, J. (1990) *Youth and the Condition of Britain: Images of Adolescent Conflict*, Athlone Press Ltd.

Davis, R. (1984) 'Living Liturgically: The Charismatic Contribution' in D. Martin and P. Mullen (eds), *Strange Gifts?* Basil Blackwell Publisher Ltd.

Enroth, R.M., Ericson, E.E. and Peters, C.B. (1972) *The Story of the Jesus People: A Factual Survey*, Paternoster Press.

Fraser, I. (1985) 'Beginnings at Dunblane' in R. Leaver and J. H. Litton (eds), *Duty and Delight: Routley Remembered: a Memorial Tribute to Eric Routley, 1917-1982*, Canterbury Press, Norwich.

Friends of After the Fire (1999a) *ATF Gig Chronology* [internet]. Available from: <http://friends.afterthefire.co.uk/atfgigs.htm> [Accessed 09 May 2007].

Friends of After the Fire (1999b) *ATF Interviews* [internet]. Available from: <http://friends.afterthefire.co.uk/atfinterviews.htm> [Accessed 09 May 2007].

Friskics-Warren, B. (2005) *I'll Take You There: Pop Music and the Urge for Transcendence*, The Continuum International Publishing Group Inc.

France, R.T. (1985), *Matthew*, Inter-Varsity Press.

Frith, S. (1983) *Sound Effects: Youth, Leisure, and the Politics of Rock 'n' Roll*, Constable, London.

Frith, S. and Horne, H. (1987) *Art into Pop*, Methuen & Co.

Game for a Laugh (2001) *Game for a Laugh* [internet]. Available from: <http://en.wikipedia.org/wiki/Game_for_a_Laugh> [Accessed 29 May 2007].

Green, J. (1998) *All Dressed Up: The Sixties and the Counterculture*, Pimlico.

Greenbelt Festival (1999) *Greenbelt from the Beginning* [internet]. Available from: <http://www.greenbelt.org.uk/?s=33> [Accessed 21 May 2007].

Haley, J.M. and Francis, L.J. (2006) *British Methodism: What Circuit Ministers Really Think*, Epworth.

Harker, D. (1992) 'Still Crazy After all These Years: What *was* Popular Music in the 1960s' in B. Moore-Gilbert and J. Seed (eds), *Cultural Revolution?: The Challenge of the Arts in the 1960s*, Routledge.

Harry, B. (2004) 'When we were very Young' in P. Trynka, P. (ed.), *The Beatles: Ten Years that Shook the World*, Dorling Kindersley Ltd.

Hastings, A. (2001) *A History of English Christianity* 1920-2000, SCM Press.

Henderson, S. (1984) *Greenbelt: Since the Beginning*, Last Minute Publications.

Hempton, D. (2005) *Methodism: Empire of the Spirit*, Yale University Press.

Hobsbawn, E. (1994) *The Age of Extremes: 1914-1991*, Abacus.

Hoggart, R. (1957) *The Uses of Literacy*, Pelican Books.

Hollandsworth, D. (2005) *A Decade of Jesus Music 1969-1979* [internet]. Available from: <http://www.one-way.org/jesusmusic/index.htm> [Accessed 25 April 2007].

Hughes, R. (1965) Music in Church, *Musical Times*, Vol.106, No.1473.

Jasper, T. (1984) *Jesus and the Christian in a Pop Culture*, London: Robert Royce Ltd.

Jones, I. and Webster, P. (2006) 'The Theological Problem of Popular Music for Worship' in Contemporary Christianity, *Crucible*, July-September 2006.

Jones, I. and Webster, P. (2006) 'Anglican "Establishment" Attitudes to "Pop" Church Music in England, c1956-1990' in K. Cooper and J. Gregory (eds), *Elite and Popular Religion: Studies in Church History.42*, Ecclesiastical History Society.

Kaan, F. (1969) 'For the Healing of the Nations' in Proprietors of Hymns Ancient and Modern, *100 Hymns for Today*, London: Clowes.

Kingsway Music (1981) *Something is seriously wrong with Christian music*, Kingsway Music Ltd.

Kingsway Publications (2003) *Songs of Fellowship Books 1-3*, Eastbourne, Kingsway Publications.

Kendrick, G. (2003) 'Worship in Spirit and in Truth' in S. Darlington and A. Kreider (eds), *Composing Music for Worship*, Canterbury Press, Norwich.

Kendrick, G. with Price, C. (2001) *Behind the Songs*, Kevin Mayhew, Ltd.

Larkin, C. (2002a) *The Virgin Encyclopedia of 60s Music*, Muze, UK, Ltd

Larkin, C. (2002b) *The Virgin Encyclopedia of 70s Music*, Muze, UK, Ltd

Lawson-Johnston, P. (1989) 'Power in Praise – Worship, 'Cloud' and the Bible' in R. Sheldon (ed.), *In Spirit and in Truth*, Hodder & Stoughton.

Lewisohn, M. (2004) 'I Wanna be your Fan' in P. Trynka, P. (ed.), *The Beatles: Ten Years that Shook the World*, Dorling Kindersley Ltd.

Livin Blues (2007) *Sister Rosetta Tharpe* [internet]. Available from: <http://www.livin blues.com/bluesrooms/sisterrosettatharpe.asp> [Accessed 30 April 2007].

Long, A. (2004) *Into the Light* [internet]. Available from: <http:www.btinternet.com/~third.bass/outofdarkness.html> [Accessed 01 April 2007].

Lynch, G. (2005) *Understanding Theology and Popular Culture*, Blackwell Publishing.

MacDonald, I. (1998) *Revolution in the Head: the Beatles' Records and the Sixties*, Pimlico.

Martin, D. (2002) *Christian Language and its Mutations*, Ashgate Publishing Ltd.

Martin, P.J. (1995) *Sounds and Society: Themes in the Sociology of Music*, Manchester University Press.

Martin, L. and Segrave, K. (1988) *Anti-rock: The Opposition to Rock 'n' Roll*, Hamden, Conn.: Archon Books.

Marwick, A. (1998) *The Sixties*, Oxford University Press.

Melly, G. (1970) *Revolt into Style: The Pop Arts in Britain*, Penguin Press.

Methodist Church (1969) *Hymns and Songs*, Methodist Publishing House.

Methodist Church (1983) *Hymns and Psalms, A Methodist and Ecumenical Hymn Book*, Methodist Publishing House.

Miles, B. (2004) *Hippie*, Cassell Illustrated.

Millington, J. (1964) *Something's Missin'* [internet]. Available from: <http://www.liv.ac.uk-qu04/crossbeats/songs.htm> [Accessed 08 July 2005].

Mission England Praise (1983) *Mission Praise*, Marshall, Morgan and Scott, Basingstoke.

Mullen, P. (1984) 'Confusion Worse Confounded' in D. Martin and P. Mullen (eds), *Strange Gifts?* Basil Blackwell Publisher Ltd.

Nadorozny, E. (2005) *The Pilgrims – Telling Youth, The Truth: Interview with Derrick Phillips* [internet]. Available from: < http//one-way.org/jesusmusic/index.html> [Accessed 30 March 2005].

Nadorozny, E. (2007) *A Beginners Guide to Christian Beat Music* [internet]. Available from: <http://www.ready-steady-go.org.uk/Christian beat.htm> [Accessed 23 March 2007].

Napier-Bell, S. (2001) *Black Vinyl White Powder*, London: Ebury Press.

Noakes, R. (1984) 'The Instinct of the Herd' in D. Martin and P. Mullen (eds), *Strange Gifts?* Basil Blackwell Publisher Ltd.

Notting Hill Music Group (1965) *Songs from Notting Hill*, Notting Hill Group Ministry.

Notting Hill Group Ministry (1972) *More Songs from Notting Hill*, Almorris Press Ltd.

Official Larry Norman UK Website (2004) *Larry in the UK* [internet]. Available from: <http://www.larrynorman.uk.com/inuk.htm> [Accessed 04 May 2007].

Osgerby, B. (1998) *Youth in Britain Since 1945*, Blackwell Publishers Ltd.

Palmer, R. (1996) *Dancing in the Street*, BBC Publications.

Page, N. (2004) *And now let's move into a time of nonsense: Why Worship Songs are Failing The Church*, Authentic Media.

Plankton Records (2005) *Out of Darkness* [internet]. Available from: <http://www.planktonrecords.co.uk/artist4.htm > [Accessed 02 April 2007].

Powell, M.A. (2002) *Encyclopedia of Contemporary Christian music*, Hendrikson Publishers, Inc.

Pulkingham, B. and Harper, J. (1978) *Combined Sound of Living Waters – Fresh Sounds*, Hodder & Stoughton.

Proprietors of Hymns Ancient and Modern (1969) *100 Hymns for Today*, Clowes and Sons Ltd.

Rees, R.L.D. (1993) *Weary and Ill at Ease*, Gracewing Books.

Robinson, J. (1963) *Honest to God*, SCM Press.

Rosman, D. (2003) *The Evolution of the English Churches 1500-2000*, University Press, Cambridge.

Routley, E. (1964) *Twentieth Century Church Music*, London: Herbert Jenkins.

Routley, E. (1982) *Christian Hymns Observed*, Prestige Publications, Inc.

Scott, K. (2003) *Archivist (third edition): A Collectors Guide to Vintage Vinyl Jesus Music 1965-1980*, Ken Scott, PO Box 110, Worthington OH 43085.

Sandbrook, D. (2006) *White Heat*, Little Brown.

Shuker, R. (1994) *Understanding Popular Music*, Routledge.

Sinclair, J. (1992) *Keeping in Tune with Heaven: A Response to the Report of the Archbishops' Commission on Church Music*, Grove Books Ltd.

Smith, P.D. (ed.) (1967) *Faith and Folk, and Clarity*, Galliard Ltd.

Sounes, H. (2001) *Down the Highway: The Life of Bob Dylan*, Doubleday.

Steven, J. (1989) *Worship in the Restoration Movement*, Grove Books Ltd.

Street, J. (1986) *Rebel Rock: The Politics of Popular Music*, Basil Blackwell Ltd

Street, J. (1992) Shock Waves: 'The Authoritative Response to Popular Music' in D. Strinati, and S. Wagg (eds), *Come on Down?: Popular Media Culture in Post-war Britain*, Routledge.

Stringfellow, J. and Stringfellow, B. (1967) 'Fair Shares for All' in P.D. Smith (ed.), *Faith, Folk and Clarity*, Galliard Ltd.

The English Hymnal Company (1975) *English Praise*, Oxford University Press.

The United Reformed Church in England and Wales (1975) *New Church Praise*, The Saint Andrews Press.

Tidball, D.J. (1994) *Who are the Evangelicals?* Marshall Pickering.

Turner, S. (1988) *Hungry for Heaven: Rock and Roll and the Search for Redemption*, Kingsway Publications Ltd.

Turner, S. (2005) *Cliff Richard: The Biography*, Lion Hudson Plc.

Turner, S. (2006) *The Gospel According to The Beatles*, Westminster John Knox Press.

Trynka, P. (ed.) (2004) The Beatles: *Ten Years that Shook the World*, Dorling Kindersley Ltd.

Wald, G.F. (2007) *Shout, Sister, Shout! The Untold Story of Rock-and-Roll Trailblazer Sister Rosetta Tharpe*, Beacon Press, Boston.

Walker, A. (1998) *Restoring the Kingdom*, Guildford: Eagle.

Ward, P. (1996) *Growing up Evangelical*, SPCK.

Ward, P. (2005) *Selling Worship*, Paternoster Press.

Webb, S.H. (2006) *Dylan Redeemed: From Highway 61 to Saved*, Continuum International Publishing Group Ltd.

Westermeyer, P. (1998) *Te Deum: The Church and Music*, Augsberg Fortress.

Wicke, P. (1987) *Rock Music*, Cambridge University Press.

Williamson, N. (2004) *The Rough Guide to Bob Dylan*, Rough Guides Ltd.

Wilson-Dickson, A. (1992) *A Brief History of Christian Music*, Lion Publishing Plc.

Wren, B. (2000) *Praying Twice: The Music and Words of Congregational Singing*, Westminster John Knox Press.

Select Discography

After the Fire (1978, reissue 2004) *Signs of Change*, Rapid.

After the Fire (1979) *Laser Love*, CBS.

Beach Boys (1966, reissue 2000) *Pet Sounds*, Capitol Records.

Beatles The (1967, reissue 1992) *Sgt. Pepper's Lonely Hearts Club Band*, Parlophone.

Beatles The (1973, reissue 1993) *The Beatles 1962-1966*, EMI Records.

Beatles The (1973, reissue 1993) *The Beatles 1967-1970*, EMI Records.

Byrds The (1997) *The Very Best of the Byrds*, Sony Music Entertainment.

Caedmon (1978) *Caedmon*, English Garden.

Cloud (1982) *Hallowed Ground*, Kingsway Music, Eastbourne.

Cream (1995) *The Very Best of Cream*, Polygram International Music.

Dylan, Bob (1963, reissue 2003) *The Freewheelin' Bob Dylan*, Sony Music Entertainment.

Dylan, Bob (1965, reissue 2003) *Highway 61 Revisited*, Sony Music Entertainment.

Dylan, Bob (1966, reissue 2003) *Blonde on Blonde*, Sony Music Entertainment.

Fisherfolk (1974) *Sound of Living Waters*, Celebration (ASCAP).

Forerunners The (1968) *Forerunners*, MGO: Key Records.

Genesis (2004) *Platinum Collection*, Virgin Records Ltd.

Haworth, Bryn (2004) *Let the Days go by/Sunny Side of the Street*, Gottdiscs.

Haworth, Bryn (1978) *Grand Arrival*, A&M.

Hendrix, Jimi (1968, reissue 1997) *Electric Ladyland*, MCA.

Hewitt, Garth (1973) 'The People of the West (Amos rides again)' in G. Hewitt (2003) *30 Songs Spanning 30 years: 1973-2003*, ICC Studios Eastbourne.

Hewitt, Garth (1976) *Love Song for the Earth*, Myrrh.

Hewitt, Garth (2003) *30 Songs Spanning 30 years: 1973-2003*, ICC Studios Eastbourne.

Ishmael & Andy (1973) *Ready Salted*, Myrrh.

Kendrick, Graham (2003) *Sacred Journey*, Make Way Music.

Love Song (1995) *Welcome Back*, Tommy Coomes.

MacKenzie Judy (1970) *Judy*, MGO: Key Records

Malcolm & Alwyn (1973) *Fools Wisdom*, Pye Records UK.

Malcolm & Alwyn (1974, reissue 1999) *Wildwall*, Footstep Recordings, Inc.

Maranatha Music (1997) *The Praise Album: Praise 1*, The Corinthian Group.

Narnia (1974) *Aslan is Not a Tame Lion*, Word Records.

Norman, Larry (1969, reissue 2002) *Upon This Rock*, Solid Rock Records.

Norman, Larry (1972, reissue 2004) *Only Visiting this Planet*, Solid Rock Records.

Norman, Larry (1973) *So Long ago the Garden*, MGM Records Inc.

Norman, Larry (1976) *In Another Land*, Solid Rock.

Norman, Larry (1981) *Something New Under the Son*, Solid Rock.

Out of Darkness (1970) *Out of Darkness*, MGO: Key Records.

Parchment (2004) *Simply Parchment: Light up the Fire*, Kingsway Music, Eastbourne.

Pilgrims The (2004) *Telling Youth the Truth*, LRL Herald.

Rolling Stones The (2005) *Forty Licks*, UMTV.

Richard, Cliff (1978) *Small Corners*, EMI.

Snell, Adrian (1980) *The Passion*, Kingsway Music, Eastbourne.

Stonehill, Randy (1976, reissue 2003) *Welcome to Paradise*, Solid Rock Records.

Various Artists (1969) *Alive*, MGO: Key Records.

Various Artists (1970) *Sound Vision in Concert*, MGO: Key Records.

Various Artists, (1979) *Greenbelt Live!* Marshalls MRT.

Various Artists (2002) *The Birth of the Blues*, Union Square Music.

Various Artists (2003) *Beginners Guide to Folk Music*, Demon Music Ltd.

Various Artists (2004) *60 Songs of Praise and Worship*, Kingsway Music, Eastbourne.

Various Artists (2005) *Mod Classics*, Demon Music Group Ltd.

Various Artists (2005) *More Best Worship Songs Ever!* Virgin EMI.

Various Artists (2006) *Christian Rhythm Festival*, Ed Nadorozny.

Yes (1991) *Yesstory*, Atlantic Recording Corporation.

Newspapers and Magazines

Buzz magazine

Church Times

Christian Herald

NME Originals, Bob Dylan and the Folk Boom 1964-1974, Volume 2, Issue 2, Tammi Iley.

Methodist Recorder

New Christian

Q Special Edition, From Elvis to the Beatles, EMAP Metro Ltd.

Q Special Edition, February 2005: Psychedelic! How Hendrix, The Beatles & Pink Floyd Turned on, EMAP Metro Ltd.

Printed in the United Kingdom
by Lightning Source UK Ltd.
132623UK00001B/151-210/P